How I Was Able To Heal My Traumas

Traumas

The Best Story Never Told

Rosie Osorio

ISBN: 978-1-952263-51-4

Dedication

This book is dedicated to my friends and family who have given me endless love and support, and to all those kids I met in adoption centers that have inspired me.

Acknowledgments

As with everything I've done in my life, this memoir would not have been possible without the love, help, and support of many people.

I really want to thank my mother Janne Alexander, My Dad Cesar Osorio, and my siblings Carolina Osorio, Judith Osorio, David Osorio, Miguel Aranda, Jefrey Aranda, and Jose Osorio.

A special thanks to all my friends and everyone in my team who has been there with me through this journey. I have to say that I would have never written this book if it wasn't for all of them.

I want to thank all those kids that I met in the adoption centers in different countries, mainly in Colombia, where I spend more time. They were such an inspiration. I was only about 6 or 7 when I promised them I would write about my time spent with them when I was older. And so, they are the reason for this memoir.

I really want to create awareness with this memoir, that while we are complaining about anything here, like something so simple as the traffic, there are kids that are dying of hunger, scarcity of water, and rape.

Please let's be thankful for everything we have and not concentrate on the bad things.

I want to thank all the amazing people that have helped me. However, I want to thank the bad ones, too, since they were my best teachers in life.

Thank you…

And don't forget that with love we can get anything.

About the Author

Rosie Osorio is an inspired writer who loves to help people flourish in life. Her inspiration to write comes from the people around her that are living a substandard life and struggling to live a better one.

Her affection towards underprivileged people stems from her own experiences in adoption centers across Colombia, where she came across dreadful living conditions and treatment of children.

At the age of 6, Rosie promised the kids in adoption centers that someday she will write about them. This book is a materialization of that promise.

Preface

Life is not complete without suffering and struggle, for these are some of the fundamental elements that a person should learn to live with. These are the elements that complete one's life by making them mature and giving them a sense of empathy.

Rosie Osorio's heartfelt story begins in 1983, Peru, and ends in America, where she got to live her life-long dream. This journey from Peru to America is not an ordinary one. It encompasses emotions, loss, abuse, suffering, hunger, and experiences in 12 adoption centers.

This story delivers a clear message: life throws curveballs at you. It's not complete without the challenges that come with it. If you are in despair, know that this time in your life shall pass too. Life changes for everyone, and if you have hope, it changes for the better.

Contents

Page Left Blank Intentionally

Chapter 1
Family

It was a crisp sunny day in 1985. A day forever etched in my memory. The day was meant for me to bask in the warmth of it like any 6-year-old, next to my brother, David. It was like any other day in the middle of the week, where I had no worries in the world. But who could have known of the catastrophe a 6-year-old and 7-year-old were to endure? Surely, no one.

First, allow me to introduce myself. I am Rosa Osorio, a woman who endured wreckage at the hands of fate. Wreckage, that tore my heart apart as a kid and left me questioning the existence of God. Today, I intend to share my journey with you, a journey of a child who only wanted to hold her Dad's hand and listen to her mum's lullabies.

As I sat to pen this story, it took me down the memory lane. As I revisited my turbulent past and reflected on it, many lessons come forth from it that I wish to share with you. This story is my journey - of loss, reunion, hope, and, most importantly, family. Family is an integral part of every living being. Parents, siblings, aunts, uncles, nieces, nephews, and grandparents. But what happens when you are forced to part ways with them? It hurts, right? It completely crushes you, the mere thought of losing a dear one. Well, I went through the same trauma at a very young age.

I know life and death are a part of life, but when you lose a family member, your heart doesn't cease to bleed. It bleeds and bleeds in agony, but you come to appease yourself with the thought of them being at a better place. I had no such pacifications when I lost someone close to me... someone I never imagined to ever part ways with. Why? Because I did not lose that person to death, but to something more profound than that. At that point, as a child, I was far too young to have fully understood the depths of the problems that swallowed my family. These problems were triggered on a sunny day in 1985.

David and I were on our way back from our school at around 1 p.m. when the sun was at its peak. We lived in Lima, Peru, and had two more sisters and a brother. Carolina was 3-years-older than me, and Judith was 4-years younger. And the smallest member of our family was Jose, who was still a baby. The sun reflected its radiance from between the trees as we raced back to our home, a past time we siblings had each day. We would race back home to the smiling face of our mother and indulge in a meal she would have fixed for us. But that day, something felt different.

David and I exchanged glances with one another as our house reeked of isolation. The lights were off, and the door shut. This was odd, I thought to myself and turned to face my elder brother, who seemed equally taken aback. We assumed that our mother was away, maybe she had gone to a store to do grocery. Confused, I suggested to David that we should seek our neighbor's assistance. If our mother was away, they might be aware of it because they were friends with our parents. Richard and Martha were our neighbors, who were always there for us.

It was a small neighborhood where everyone was almost aware of everyone's business. If someone needed a favor from someone, be it in monetary terms or food, it was provided to them. Unbeknownst to the misfortune that was about to engulf David and me, we made our way to knock on our neighbor's door. Patiently, we waited for their door to open and see familiar faces welcome us with the same smile they always had. But that day was not an ordinary one. It was meant to alter the fate of my family. Martha answered the door with furrows dented on her forehead. David was taken aback by the frown Martha was adorning. But as her eyes registered our muddled faces, her demeanor changed. Fear and hesitation crossed her eyes, and soon she was joined by Richard. Both husband and wife exchanged uneasy glances, leaving David and me to look at each other questioningly. I remember holding my brother's hand as we were invited inside by the couple. We were accustomed to visiting them, but that day it all felt out of place.

There was a shift in the energy that day, a mourning lethargy you could say. Very patiently, Martha sat both of us down, looking at us as if we were precious China, and her words could break us. And maybe her words did chip our hearts later on.

"David, Rosie… did you go to your house?"

"We did, Martha. Mom isn't there. Do you know where Mom went?" I asked as David was far too anxious to speak. I was also growing bothered by this sudden unnerving feel. It was as if your subconscious is aware of a predicament about to unfurl and starts to prepare you by making you nervous. I was feeling just the same. I wanted Martha to answer me immediately so David and I could quickly head back home and be comfortable within our walls.

"Rosie, David, your Mom isn't here." It was a simple answer Martha gave that almost immediately knocked the air out of our lungs. After all, we were just little kids.

Immediately my mind started to burst with concern. "Then where is she? Where is our Mom? Do you know where she went? Did she go to the grocery store?"

"No, honey… she didn't."

"Then where is she?" At this point, David and I were agitated. What were these adults rambling about? Why wouldn't they tell us what had happened?

"Rosie, David, your mother has left. She won't be coming back." Martha shakily answered.

It seemed someone had commanded my heart to stop beating. I looked at David, whose face had turned pale. We were horrified and wanted to know if something terrible had happened to her, but Martha was only speaking to us cautiously, and it perturbed me. "What do you mean? Mom isn't coming back?"

"Rosie, David, honey, before I tell you where your Mom is, I need the two of you to promise me not to tell your Dad about any of this, alright? You have to swear that no matter what happens, you won't tell your Dad a word?"

"Why?" David and I questioned together. Why was there a need for us to hide something from Dad? A little insight about me here is that I had always been my Daddy's princess. My Dad was the greatest man to me, and why shouldn't he be? He adored my siblings and me to bits. He loved us and never did us wrong. Well, except for hurting Mom.

My father was a very doting man, and my mother was just the same, but they had differences. Maybe they had run out of love for each other. My father was a raging alcoholic, which made loving him harder. He would come home drunk and would start abusing and beating my mother. My mother never gave him any reason to hurt her physically, but he would bash her and beat her black and blue. All that beating must have affected her mentally. As a child, I could never perceive her trauma to be this deep. But now, I understand why my Mom did what she did.

As a child, I did not like how my Dad used to beat my Mom, but he was still my Dad, and I loved him. I could never understand how he used to adore us and then hurt my Mom physically to no end.

Martha looked at us worriedly as she was still struggling to find the right words. "Rosie, David, your mother has left. She was unable to withstand the abuse any longer. She was tired of getting hurt repeatedly. She couldn't stand your Dad beating her anymore, so she left."

"Left? Where did Mom go? Tell me, where is my Mom?" I was on the verge of bursting into tears. At this point, David was numb. In just one day, our world had shattered, and we failed to understand how this could happen to us.

"She is trying to get to the U.S. Your Mom is going from country to country to reach America, but she will be coming back for the two of you, honey. Just don't tell your Dad. You know he gets angry. Your Mom will come back soon for you, don't worry."

Even as Martha tried to console us, it did not matter. David and I were only kids who were told their mother had left for good. I couldn't stop crying. Why had my Mom left?

Had it gotten that bad? And did she even think of David and me before she was stepping out of the door?

Sometime later, I calmed myself with a false hope Martha had given David and me that Mom would come back sometime soon to get us. I faced my brother and saw his eyes were red and swollen, and his cheeks were tear-stained. I gathered it was just the two of us now since Mom had taken Carolina, Judith, and Jose with her. The next thing I remember is David telling me with fear in his eyes, "Rosie, Dad will be reaching home any time soon."

We gathered our stuff and scampered off from our neighbors to reach our home. For us, the loss we just incurred was of little significance compared to the sheer thought of our Dad's wrath. He would return home, possibly intoxicated. If he found out in a drunken state what had happened, he would wreak havoc. Thus, David and I were burdened with the trouble of finding a way to tackle our Dad, who was expected to return home within an hour or two.

Instead of playing with toys, we fumbled with a broom to dust and sweep. We quickly changed out of our uniforms to ensure they would not be stained by dirt and cleaned the house before our Dad arrived. In the heat of the moment, my brother and I divided chores. While he took care of cleaning our house, I surrendered myself to the kitchen, hoping to cook rice. How hard it could have been, I thought to myself. I had watched Mom prepare rice countless times before, hence I concluded it wouldn't be much of a hassle.

I made the rice. They were terrible, completely burnt. The smell of burnt rice diffused in the entire house, along with our dread. Not to mention, I had added half a cup of salt in the rice, ensuring they were completely inedible. With each passing second, my heart palpitations became louder out of fear of facing Dad? To make matters worse for ourselves, we were to pretend we didn't know what had happened and where our Mom was. That surely added weight to our little minds.

It didn't take long for my Dad to figure out something was not right the moment he stepped in. I could barely move in Dad's presence, and David stood rooted to his spot as well. One look at us, and Dad knew Mom was missing. He must have smelled the burned rice.

"Where is your Mom?" His voice was stern at first, but our trembling lips softened his demeanor. His shoulders hung a little loose than their previous rigid state when he repeated the question.

"We don't know, Dad." I nervously answered. He must have believed me right then because his eyes were no longer dark. I could see the worry in them now.

"Did you ask the neighbors?" His voice was trembling a little. The authority in it had evaporated into thin air.

"We asked. They don't know Dad. Mom wasn't here when we came from school."

It hurt me to be lying to the man whose shell crumbled in front of my eyes. Dad ran his hands on his face at the sudden obstacle life had thrust our way.

"I want the two of you to lock the door. I am going to go look for Jane, ok?" Dad assured us, but I was far too worried. I did not want to lose him.

"No, Dad!"

"I will be back, Rosie. Stay with your brother and lock the door, alright?"

Even in his intoxicated state, my Dad went out that night and returned late. He was exasperated when he returned. I remember his swollen eyes and dejection sprawled on his face. He was not the man I was used to seeing, and it made me cry all over again. Tears welled up in my eyes, and as much as I wanted to fight them, as much as I tried to keep them at bay, they flowed down my cheek profusely. That night, the three of us wept in darkness and silence.

We skipped school the next day, and Dad missed his work just to go and look for Mom all over Lima again. To see his face the following day was a consolation I never knew I needed, and I felt at ease even though our house was starting to haunt with the missing presence of Mom and my siblings. Dad had gone from neighbor to neighbor, asking if someone was aware where Mom could have gone, but each one of them lied. They lied straight to his face.

No one told him where his wife was. No one helped him. They all withheld the truth from him as he frantically searched for my mother in the town. The neighbors deemed it acceptable for my mother to run away from the troublesome marriage. Thus, none of them wanted to ease the woe of my father. It was as if they were amused to see him in such a miserable state.

It infuriated me to see my Dad knocking on each door, and I hated myself more for not telling him the truth. I failed to understand the reason why I had to lie to my Dad back then about where Mom was. The day after my Mom disappeared seemed long, I felt each second of each minute of each hour tick away. My eyes were focused on the door in hopes of seeing the face of either one of my parents. Finally, when Dad came home late at night, his sight was one of absolute devastation. His life was torn apart, and he was ruined. I could see in his eyes he knew the reason why. The reason why Mom was gone, he knew it was because of him.

Every day, my Dad would leave to look for my mother in hospital hallways and morgues. Each nook and cranny that he drove past in Lima, he only searched for the face of my Mom and would return home at the end of the day defeated. He was defeated, and it hurt me. For some odd reason, I seemed to have accepted the harsh reality that my Mom would not be coming back for David and me. Maybe she left us with Dad to take care of him, while she took Carolina, Judith, and Jose. My tears dried up as I watched my Dad cry each night while pouring himself drink after drink.

I wanted to comfort my father, but my lips were sealed with a promise. I did not have it in me to be breaking the promise I made to Martha. Alas... David and I were left stranded. The little joy we had was drained from our lives. Only pain and remorse lingered around our house. Our family was torn, and everything started slipping from our grasp. As if the worry of my Mom and siblings' whereabouts was not enough, I now had to worry about my Dad's deteriorating state as well. I was left to watch my father utterly helpless and cry himself to sleep each night after having poured unlimited drinks.

It is hard to recall how David and I survived, how we had our meals on time. I guess my memory about sustenance is a bit hazy, as all that echoes within my mind are my own suppressed sobs, unuttered apologies, and my Dad's hysteria. There was no more happiness left. Even when we had tried to comfort Dad, it did not matter. He would spend his days in the futile hunt to find Mom, and his nights mourning our loss. Day and night, I watched my father slip into oblivion. I watched him fall into the abyss of depression.

I could have placed my Dad out of his misery by confessing that I was aware of Mom's whereabouts and why she left us all. But I didn't. And it did not matter either. As Dad's state deteriorated, someone broke the news to him. Be it out of mercy or for further amusement to see how he would react; someone told Dad that Mom had gone to the U.S. to be far from him. He had broken her beyond repair. For Dad, this phase of mourning was far more devastating than the previous one. Each night he would cry with a drink in his hand, feeling sorry for having hurt Mom, "Come back, Jane. I am sorry for hurting you. I love you. I am sorry I hurt you so bad, Jane."

I would run to my room to shed tears watching my Dad in pain. Where was my Mom? Did she miss us or not? My brother and I were yet to hear from her. It had been nearly six months now. Six months since she was gone, and through this entire time, I watched my father die a little each day. He seemed no less than a breathing corpse on whom grey clouds loomed and thundered endlessly. As his drinking intensified, my Dad developed another destructive habit – he turned borderline suicidal. The pain must have been unbearable for him.

One night he was in the kitchen, drinking as per usual. I saw him close his eyes to the melody of a sad song, letting his tears flow. I remember the tremble of his lips and how I wanted to wipe his tears away and comfort him. But I watched him helplessly, hiding behind the doorway panel.

My own tears were cascading down my cheek. The song continued to mortify me as my Dad cried more and more. I never knew a person could cry so much, but it seemed his heart had taken a plunge.

Only to prove my worst fear right, Dad pulled a knife from the kitchen drawer. I gasped and felt as though someone had pulled the ground from beneath my feet as I watched my Dad mercilessly drag the sharp blade across his wrist with his trembling hand. My voice seemed to have drowned at the back of my throat. The oozing blood smeared the kitchen tiles, and then my Dad collapsed. That was when I found my voice and yelled, DAD!

My body jerked as I cried until David came running to the scene. I watched him tremble, too, before I ran out to bring back someone to help us. My feet had carried me to the door of our priest, and it did not take him long to realize something dreadful had happened as we ran back together to see my Dad crying and quivering in pain. The Father ran to his side and pulled him up before slapping him to consciousness. The smack of his palm echoed through the empty walls of our house until his anger broke the silence. "Are you insane? Are you this weak? Do you not see your kids? Huh? Do you not see them crying? Are you blind to their needs? They need you. They need a parent! They need their father!"

The Father helped my Dad up and cleaned his wound. He bandaged it before putting my Dad to sleep after explaining to him how we still needed him. I remember the pool of blood that was in the kitchen and my Dad's whispers of an apology. I stayed up the whole night, wondering if something would go wrong. I was afraid to rest my eyes for even a second, fearing I would lose my Dad too. But you have to go through a storm before the rainbow would appear.

The next morning, my Dad came to us with a frown on his face, and tears lacing his eyes. But he did not shed them; he only embraced us tightly and apologized for having ignored us all this while. That day, I saw a flicker of hope once again. I saw his eyes shine a little when he saw David and me. Our Dad was no longer drunk or breaking apart, and this was enough for us. We accepted our fate, and whatever it had in store for us, as long as we were getting our Dad back. I remember hugging my Dad tightly, afraid he would slip away from my grip, but he wrapped his arms around me and comforted me. "Don't worry, Rosie. I am here. It will be alright, baby." And I trusted him completely.

From that very day, I watched my father make an effort for David and me. Naturally, he was accustomed to drinking to ease his plight, but he tried to reduce that. He tried to learn and cook for us, so David and I were always fed. And I grew proud of my Dad. He loved us, and we loved him back. We became each other's support system. We were there for one another. If my Dad cried, I would wipe his tears and tell him everything was alright. I would hold his hand, and he would believe me. And when either David or I would cry, he would hold us in his arms and cradle us to sleep.

Our broken hearts began to mend slowly. We took steps forward to accept reality and moved on. It had been nearly a year since Mom was gone. We had not heard from her but never stopped hoping that one day she would come for us.

My Dad learned how to be stronger for us. He learned to be the father that he failed to be before. He became our protector. I could feel happiness radiate once more, the walls in our house no longer echoed cries and pleas. Dad was trying to fix his home, his family. It is odd how life works. At one moment, it's breaking, and the other it's showering you with mercy. And you fail to comprehend what is actually happening? You fail to understand if an unexpected blessing is your solace after having endured endless trauma. Just when Dad was working hard to amend things, a year nearly after that unfaithful summer day, he received a letter. It was a letter from Mom. It was a letter announcing her homecoming, stating how she had never made it to the U.S. and that she was coming back with our siblings.

It was news of bliss. I remember how our sad faces lit up with smiles. I was on cloud nine. Mom was coming back. My Mom would come back, and I would run to her arms and feel her warmth again. My siblings were coming, my sisters and brothers. David and I would be able to play with them again. Dad was better now. More than better, if truth be told. Maybe we could all go on a picnic, I thought to myself.

Elevated, I pranced around the neighborhood, announcing the arrival of my Mom. My lips started to hurt from all the smiling, but it felt as if we had crossed a hurricane and were getting closer to safer waters. But an ocean is an ocean. It is neither a friend nor a foe. Little did I know that my family was not cut for a happy ever after. And that life only rendered us moments of fabricated bliss.

Chapter 2
Daddy's Little Girl

I was happy. But what happiness is complete without sadness? See, bliss and plight share a special bond, one where they shadow the other. You will always find happiness in sadness and pain in joy. The entire prospect of being reunited with my family and having my siblings and mother back was enough to leave me soaring in the sky. When the day arrived, our house reeked of celebration. We did not need to string festive lights around our house, for our hearts were lit up with glee. I had fathomed for the day to be a reward from God for having endured immense pain. Alas, I could never have imagined even in my nightmare what was about to unfold.

My Mom was happy. The house roared with the cheery laughter of my siblings and me. My Dad's eyes gleamed with affection, and a smile of being complete was perched on his lips. My mother maintained a distance from him. However, she could not help but hold David and me close to her chest. From their tiring bus rides to the stopovers she had, her story was a treat for David and me. We would be lost in a daze, listening to the stories intently, being overwhelmed with a sense of having lived the journey ourselves. To see her so quiet around Dad was unnerving. Her eyes were indifferent toward him while his were always shining with tenderness. Each time he tried to approach her, she would busy herself. While he would be at work in the daytime, my mother would be herself.

My mum seemed to have repressed her emotions. But if someone took a deeper look, they would have been able to trace the scars she inherited from her marriage to my Dad. The scars that were fiery scarlet, and it was only a matter of time before they would make their appearance. Slow at first, as my parents started to argue. Dad knew Mom was distant, and while he gave her time, he sought her forgiveness too. Only, my mother was adamant about not even glancing his way, and it broke him apart. With time, their emotions started to take a toll on them. Their emotions started to spill, posing a threat to the fragile thread that had restrung my family together.

See, Dad was happy too, but his happiness did not define the state of my Mom, who was still gravely wounded by the abuse she had suffered. The abuse had left her broken, and she did not want to seek happiness from this house any longer. All his efforts to sober up and fix the house bit by bit proved to be a waste because all she could see and hear were her trapped sobs. Each day haunted her, and that terrified me. There was an aura of suffocating tension in our house, thick enough to be sliced by words. But she never rendered her words to ease this suffering of ours. She was unknowingly inflicting the suffering on all of us, and not just Dad.

Sometime later, after my Dad failed to reconcile his differences with Mom, she approached me one night. I was tossing and turning, fighting this dread that was already creeping up my neck. The house was doused in eerie silence.

"Rosa? Rosa, are you awake?" My mother's soft voice came through the door.

I immediately shot up, sitting straight in bed, and looking at her with privy eyes. I watched her make her way to me and draping her arms around me. Instantly, I melted in her hold, closing my eyes briefly and thanking God under my breath for blessing me with both my parents. If only I would have known what was to come, then perhaps I would have flinched from her touch instead of seeking comfort in her hold. She made me rest my head on her lap, and I did, closing my eyes as she ran her fingers across my scalp. It was magical, her touch, how it wiped away all my worries by the simplest of a gesture.

"Rosa, baby, there is something I need to talk to you about." She gently cooed, and I remained silent, allowing her voice to be my lullaby. I was starting to drift into slumber when her next set of words left me rigid. *"But you have to promise me not to tell your Dad, ever. Ok, baby?"*

What was it with people telling me to lie to my Dad? It had already been difficult for me to keep the truth away from my Dad, and I had to watch him suffer in pain. But I remained quiet, my sleep all gone now. *"You and David are leaving with me."*

"Leaving?" I asked. Part intrigued and part wondering why we not to tell Dad if we were leaving?

"Yes, baby." She took a pause. I was able to hear her draw in a sharp breath within the cloaking of the silence of the night. *"We are leaving. But you cannot tell your Dad, ok? Honey, I know you are strong, and you understand. You understand, baby, that mama is not happy with your Dad anymore. He hurt me, Rosa…"*

This time, I moved away from my mother's hold, my eyes threatening to bulge out of their sockets in understanding. She intended to leave Dad alone and again.

"Mom, no…" I whimpered. I did not know why tears were forming in my eyes. It only seemed my mind was mirroring my mother's distress. *"Why can I not tell Dad? Are we not taking him with us?"*

Hesitation flickered in her eyes as I received my answer. I moved back, but she gently held me with my hands to pull me closer to her. She ran her hand across my cheeks before cupping them tenderly.

"Rosa, baby, your Dad hurt me, and I cannot take him with me."

"I don't want to go without Daddy," I tried to fight her, but my voice betrayed me.

Mom closed her eyes, a tear escaping her cheek. *"Rosa, don't worry. I know you love your Daddy. But we have to go this time, for real. We are just going to go and visit your grandparents, and then you can visit your Dad. Promise me, Rosa, you won't tell your Dad."*

Desperation laced her voice. I could see the hurt shattering her as she said the words. I was left to push down the forming lump in my throat, fighting my emotions that were wreaking my sanity. I wanted to ask my Mom why she was being so cruel to me. If she knew I loved Dad, then why was she asking me to go away from him? And, if I was coming back to visit him, then why was I to hide it from him? At the moment, my heart skipped a beat, acknowledging there was more to what she said, but to see her breaking before me, I succumbed to her desires.

My Mom did not want me to express my emotions to Dad. Else, he would have seen through the charade I was instructed to put up. It hurt me when I saw my Dad, knowing I was to leave him in a few days without telling him. My head told me not to tell him, but my heart told me otherwise. The dilemma I was treading soon took a toll on my health, and this was the first time I was introduced to a panic attack. I was far too young, but life did not spare me an ounce of mercy.

A night before we were set to leave, our bags packed and tucked away from my Dad's sighting, my lungs finally caved in. They weighed heavy with the burden of holding back. My eyes that were forced to stay dry finally shed the hurt I was piling up. Tears started flowing down my cheeks. I wanted to tell Daddy that we were leaving him. Instead, I watched him lurch toward me that night, seeing how I was fighting a battle within myself. I was with him yet felt the miles that were to come between us.

"Rosa? Are you alright? What's the matter?"

His concern still haunts me, as it did back then. His words were ringing in my ears and prevented me from drowning in misery. He was quick to hold me in his arms, to pat my back. I remember him wiping my tears away and kissing me on my forehead, chanting me a comfort he did not know was to be in vain. He told me that everything was alright, but his eyes were full of fear like mine. He was scared, and so was I. The only difference was I knew why I was scared while he was helpless and unequipped with the truth. That night, he stayed up with me, ensuring that I was tucked safely to sleep. He was distraught and fell asleep next to me.

The next morning came rolling in with its searing reality – we were leaving. With groggy eyes, I woke up to my mum, carrying me in her arms. I vaguely remember screaming and crying, but no words came out of my mouth. My plight was inaudible, as my Dad had woken up just as quick and held me by the other hand. I can never get rid of the image of our dimly lit hallway, only the sunlight from outside seeping into the war zone cautiously. Even nature was petrified of the happening, as my parents were tugging on my arms. Each tried to pull me toward them without letting me grasp what I wanted. Yet another episode of trauma was introduced to me. Before this, I would never have known the amount of pain a human heart can endure.

My parents continued to bicker, both assuring me that everything would be alright. But that was a lie. My Mom knew what she meant by everything – she was taking us away forever. My Dad, on the other hand, was unaware of the fact and assured me that whatever it was that was hurting me would soon be fine. The more they warranted me an assurance, the more hysteric I grew because I knew what was happening. My heart was beseeching for her to grant me my voice and tell my Dad what was happening. I was his little girl, and all I wished to do was to yell out the truth at the top of my lungs, but the promise I made earlier prevented me from doing so.

"I am only taking her to the park, and then I have to go to dinner with my friend. I will stay there. You will see her in the morning."

My mum made an excuse that instantly made my Dad leave my hand, and I fell to the ground. But my tears refused to run dry. He believed the lie that came straight through her teeth and only hugged me one last time before she held me by the hand and seated me in the car with my siblings.

The ride from my house to the bus stop was quiet. My siblings and I did not dare utter a word, scared that it would deprive us of the last memory we were to have of our house and Dad. We knew our happy-ever-after was no more, and that thought alone left me crying in silence, hating my Mom, and questioning God. Why did I have to suffer? What wrong had I done not to be blessed with both my parents in life? Why was it that while I had my Dad, I could not have Mom and vice versa? The more I thought, the heavier my soul felt.

As we got off the car, and the rest of my siblings mingled with others, I held myself back. Somehow my brain had shut off, refusing to admit the reality as if it would turn back the clock and take me back to my Dad. Nonetheless, this was not bound to happen. Through my glossy eyes, what I saw next only added fuel to my blazing grief. It was Richard, and the way he held my Mom's hand sufficed to proclaim her to be his. He was the one to have replaced my Dad. It was enough to fill me with distaste and repulse for him. I could not wrap my head around the idea of him being my stepfather.

Nothing else mattered after that. My heart was numb, and all I wanted was to go back to Daddy. After boarding the bus, the buzzing energy of my siblings, who were ecstatic at the prospect of leaving, failed to ignite me with a similar passion. Instead, I turned my head away to block Richard's face from entering my peripheral and focused on the barren scenery we were passing through. My home and Dad were far away, draining me of all emotions but remorse. It is the worst sentiment one could live with. It is like poison, slowly bleeding within the system to corrupt it with nothingness. I was feeling that nothingness.

The next morning, our bus came to a halt at a bus terminal, where passengers all alighted to freshen up and purchase snacks, except for my family and me. It was when the crowd cleared from the bus, that I saw him sitting on the road. At first, I thought it was a mirage. But then, it dawned upon me. The parched lips and blotchy red skin from sitting underneath the sun did nothing to hide his puffy eyes with streaks of red in them. The hollow beneath them was a giveaway to his state of being berserk. It was my Dad. He was there.

"DAD!" I yelled and hopped in my seat before scrambling away. *"DAD! Daddy! It's my Daddy! He's here!"* I yelled, never once looking back at my Mom or siblings.

There was no worry or care. All my eyes could see was my Dad standing on his feet now, smiling amidst the waterfall of tears. He seemed to have discovered my Mom planning, knowing where the bus would be taking us next. I dove into the safety of my Dad's embrace and felt his hands tightening around me. For once, ever since we left, I felt content. He slowly moved me back, kissing my forehead, and then turned on his heels to see the lit-up faces of my siblings and the dull one of Mom. He gulped and grabbed hold of my hand as we walked onto the bus. From the window, I could see Richard ducking at the very back of the bus. Back then, I scoffed at him for being the villain. But later in my life, I understood how my Mom had fallen in love with another man who did not abuse her.

"Jane…" my Dad said breathlessly, *"please, Jane, forgive me. Please, I beg you.*

"Don't create a scene here and leave," was all my Mom could mutter. Disbelief filled my senses at how mum rejected my Dad.

"Jane, please, I beg you. Don't leave me. I need you. I need my kids. Please don't leave me," he cried. He was on his knees while my Mom was filled with resentment against him.

"I don't care! I hate you. You hurt me. You broke me. I hate you for that. I gave you many chances, and now it's over. Just go."

"No, no, no. Please, Jane. Don't leave me. I have changed, I swear. I have stopped drinking, and I promise I will fix this… our marriage, our home. Please don't take my kids away from me. I love you, Jane." My Dad continued to beg, but my Mom never once melted. Her heart had hardened, and no matter what he said now, it did not affect her the least bit.

"Just leave, alright. I hate you, and I don't want to live with you. I want to live with my family and my kids. I'm

taking my kids away to live with me. Just leave."

Her words were razor-sharp, piercing through my heart. My Dad kept on crying, and my Mom went back to take her seat. Time seemed to have stopped, and the air around us churning dread. I looked at my siblings for help, for either one of them to stand up and tell our Mom that we wanted to live with Dad too, but no one did.

By now, I had had enough. I could not see my Dad breaking apart like this. I loved Mom dearly and understood her reasons. He had hurt her so much that now she could not bear being with him. But he had never hurt anyone of us, and we were his just as much as we were hers. I wiped my tears away and turned to look at her, suddenly courage soaring within me.

"I am not going." It was a simple statement, but my Mom seemed baffled by the authority in my words.

"Rosa, we are leaving, ok." She reasserted.

"No, Mommy. I love you, Mommy, but I love Daddy too. I cannot leave him. I want to live with him, no matter what."

I did not want to leave Daddy. If I did, he would hurt himself, I cried. It seemed the earlier words had reinforced life in my father, and his face glowed. He was happy, holding me close, and Mom could see that I meant every word I said. Now her eyes misted as she watched me exchange my last goodbye with my siblings. I saw the bus move away once more, my hands nestled safely in Dad's, but my heart still clenched and unclenched in pain. The venom of a bitter farewell was pulsating throughout me. With my head hung low, I walked behind Dad, unsure if I would ever get to see my Mom or sibling ever again. All I wanted at the moment was for the ground to swallow me whole and plunge me out of this insufferable agony, but I had to force my steps to move forward.

On our way back to our home in Lima, without my mother, brothers, and sisters, I was extremely upset. Their upset faces and quivering lips haunted me on the way back home. I held tight to my Dad's side, my mind chanting only one thought – *will I ever see them again?* In spite of being flustered by my Mom's words and actions, I loved her. I loved her so much. I had witnessed her suffering and how she used to cry herself to sleep every night. Perhaps Dad deserved this? Perhaps Mom could have forgiven him? And perhaps I would have had my family together. But these were only fragments of my imagination for the time to come. My pastime, when I was alone at home, was sniffing the memories of my family hidden in every corner of every room.

I clearly remember when I was on my way home with Dad on the bus. It was night. Looking at the sky, I held the sea of stars in my eyes. Even in the darkness, the light gave me a glimmer of hope. I was resting my head on my father's laps. I could feel his sadness radiating off him despite him assuring me that everything was going to be alright. Somehow I believed him back then. My eyes were trained on the slumbering horizon above.

I told him, *"Daddy, I know. Daddy, look, it's dark now. But you can see the light in the sky."*

He responded, *"Oh yeah, what lights?"*

I replied, *"The stars, Daddy, and remember that I am here with you, and I need you too."*

My eyes shifted from the stars above to my Dad, taking note of how he, too, was looking at them now. It was no easy task to inhale the lingering smell of family that once occupied the same space. Daddy and I had to take it one hour at a time. We would look at the clock, hoping for the day to end. After a couple of weeks of being home and depressed, he resumed work and placed me in school. To divert his attention, he began to fix the house. He was not the old, frenzied drunkard man I used to know. God had changed him. We often prayed and had faith that Mom would come home, and our family would be one again.

Six months later, God answered our prayers. Mom sent a letter saying that she was coming home. She had only made it to Panama this time. In her letter, she wrote that she wanted to see us badly. Her words left Dad excited. He started getting everything ready for her. He wanted her to see that he had changed for the better. He even hired a few people to help cook and help her with the housework. She came back with my brothers and sisters. I was happy, and so was my Dad.

I told myself again for the second time, *"We are going to be a family again!"*

I had a lot of hope. I had a lot of faith. But again, everything felt apart not too long after I was sent to live at my grandparent's house. Confused and frustrated, I wondered why they would send us away just one day after

Mom arrived. My grandmother finally broke down and told me the reason they were keeping us away from our parents. It was to keep us away from witnessing the fights to come, as my mother had become pregnant from another man. All that came out from my mouth was one name - *Richard?* She nodded her head.

It was painful to know that nothing was going to mend my broken family. I had no idea what was going to happen now. I did not speak with anyone. All I asked my grandparents was when my siblings and I were going to be picked up. The only answer that came from them was one word – soon.

I remember that night how I stayed up staring out into oblivion filled with swirling threat. While I was at it, an unusual occurrence took place. I thought there was something wrong with my vision when I saw a spilling neon bluish-white light. The longer I stared at it, the bizarre it grew. I remember looking at it for long until my eyes managed to form a visage within it that I deemed to be of God. At that very moment, all of my worries were eradicated. A simple visioning of something I believed in succeeded in filling me with hope. I thought I had seen God, and now everything would be fine. The thought in itself was comforting, and my state of restlessness vanished. Soon slumber took over, and the next day, I woke up feeling calm.

Well, I did take advantage of the situation back then. My Dad's sister, Ana (a famous painter), taught me how to paint. I learned a lot from her, as I admired her incredible art so much. I just wanted to watch more of her mixing the colors and birthing newer colors from them. I have to say it is a beautiful talent to be able to create amazing paintings as she did. Later in life, I became good at it myself. Up until this day, I love to do oil painting.

You see, sometimes we never know why things happen. Later in life, my paintings became a tool to make good chunks of cash just when we needed it the most. What I am trying to say is never regret your past. We are all here to learn from the good, the bad, and the ugly. That is the best school - the school of life. It teaches us lessons that are crucial to our existence. It teaches us how to live, how to endure pain, and how to mold ourselves according to our surroundings.

Anyhow, my Mom came to pick us up the very next day while Dad was at work. This time again, she sat me down, telling me how we will be leaving.

"Rosa, we are leaving again. And I am sorry, baby, this time you won't be able to say goodbye to your Dad. I need you to promise that you won't say a word to him. Please, baby, you have to do this for me."

As my Mom packed some of our clothing, I was unable to process what was happening. It was only the second day of her arrival. Dad was away, and we left in a hurry. No warning, no final goodbyes, no safe-keeping anything except for his memories. By the time my mind grasped what had just happened, I was far away from Lima on a bus. This time, I could feel it in my bones that no matter how hard I tried to search for his face among a sea of unknown faces, I would never see my Dad again. I was right. I never saw him again. While my body was Columbia-bound, my heart and soul were homebound.

Chapter 3
San Andres

My eyes lingered on the escaping emerald trees solemnly. I could hear incoherent mumbling between the awake and snores of the slumbering passengers around me. Each turn the bus took, my heart threatened to leap out and run back to my father. From one bus stop to another, we continued traveling in anticipation of reaching a new port. There was no turning back. I knew it. Each slope the bus climbed and slipped down only increased the distance between me and home.

The only consolation I did hold within me that managed to stop my tears from flowing was David. He was still with Daddy. Daddy and David would take care of each other – this, I chanted to myself each time I needed to muster the courage to climb a different bus. Deep within my heart, however, there was a flickering ray of hope that I would get a chance to go back. It was only extinguished by the horrid breeze that whipped across my face after we crossed the border of Peru.

Through Quito, Ecuador, we weaved our way to Columbia. I woke up to the grunts of the engine and the loud chatter of the people around me. We had finally reached our destination. Just as I was willing my mind to swallow the truth, our journey that was to be ceased at Bogota further extended to Cali and then came to a rest at Medellin.

We were traveling for two weeks or more. I cannot recall precisely, for the time was a notion not applicable to me. I was in a different zone, where time did not matter, where time was not the remedy to heal the scar I unwillingly inherited. Well, apart from our caretaker Susana, a woman who barely looked at us when Mom would turn her back, people of diverse nature surrounded me. There were people with disheveled hair and straightened clothes. And then there were people with smooth hair but crinkled clothing, depicting their state of being on a voyage for too long.

People were looking at me with their curious eyes. Their bleak smiles and shrewd frowns posed a threat that led me to stay closer to my family. We felt like ducklings led by our Mom, Richard, and Susana. Even as little children, we were aware that something was wary about this new country we were traveling in. After all, back then, Medellin was in the clutches of cartels and drug lords. One of them was Pablo Escobar. Hotel to hotel, we shifted. Some hotels had seamless linen bedding, and some had bedbugs in the flimsy mattress. At times the stench of vomit would be too prominent, and sometimes the voices coming from another room were far too gruesome. Another thing I did familiarize myself with was the state of the neighborhood. It was crowded and noisy. It seemed calm and quiet were concepts that were unknown in this part of the world. I missed home more than ever. I missed the comfort of our bare walls that did not reek of hostility and fear. I missed seeing my Dad around. His mere presence used to make me feel safe, but here, it was a different story altogether. I no longer knew if I was safe. I could sense danger lurking in every corner.

Within two weeks of traveling, Mom and Richard were running out of money. It was truly ironic how life took away a stable roof away from our head, only to place us under the mercy of a rented one. And if life was not done with mocking my misery, it went on to show me a glimpse of what my future would hold. It showed me a picture of devastation, of broken vows, and of new bonds that were ridiculing the ones I knew. It reminded me of the harsh reality that my Dad was now replaced by a man he once trusted. Looking at Richard, I only wondered if things would have turned out differently between my parents, had he not been in the picture. Then I would turn to look at Mom and find my answer in her smile. In spite of all the hardships beginning to surface, her smile harbored no fear. It seemed she had found the way to her bay amidst a hurricane that intended to wreck us.

Mom and Richard shared a bed in the hotel we stayed at. He was sleeping beside her, their heartbeats resting in sync. But the sight of it was enough to traumatize me and left my heart bleeding in silence again. This was a verification of her severing all ties with Dad. The next few days to come were full of fright, worry, and panic for my family. The previous night, we had fallen asleep to screams in the eerie quiet of the night.

I remember being told to ignore the sound and try to sleep. But it was difficult. How was I to close my ears to the sound of plight? Only later through the night when the voices pleading for mercy, hushed, I had managed to close my eyes for some hours. We woke up again to an abhorring scent radiating through the block and Mom and Richard's murmurs. They were distressed. They did not need to say it out loud. We knew we were running out of money. The only question that seemed to be haunting us now was *what next?* She knew we had to go all the way to the U.S., which is why she had Susana with us as she needed the extra pair of hands to handle all of us through the excruciating journey ahead of us. How else was Mom to tackle all of us siblings, while she was expecting another child?

"How about some breakfast?" Richard asked after some time, to which our stomach affirmed by grumbling.

Unbeknown to the streets flooded with crimson blood and alleyways echoing the yelps of people, we abandoned the comfort of our hotel room in the hopes of finding food but faced a biting incident instead. We had to pass through spilled organs, the stench of torture, and monstrosity to make our way out of the neighborhood.

"It's the cartels. They killed people for money," Richard commented to my Mom as she hurdled us before moving forward. Any appetite we had was lost.

Who even does this? Does life have no value? Do hands not shake when taking the life of another? I failed to find an answer to why humanity failed to exist. I was just a little girl, yet through my eyes, I could see how prone we were to be the next victim of an ongoing rage or the sudden monstrous need of a person to assert their authority by harming the powerless. This was what went on around us for a week, a vicious cycle of falling asleep to shouts and screams I wished I could mute. And if this terror was not enough, there was the dread of not having our next meal.

My siblings were starving. Our state was frantic, our clothes dirty. Our faces covered in pollution and frown. I just wanted to go home. I wanted to tell Mom to please take us back, but we were deep in the middle of nowhere. Had it been only me who was with her, I would have been less worried about hunger. But watching my siblings starve left me helpless. Moreover, to be helpless is the worst feeling of all. It is the moment where you realize you have hands and feet, but you cannot put them to use. It is the moment when you have a heart that refuses to beat. It is to have a soul that knows no hope. I loathed this feeling. All I wanted was to secure a way of salvaging my family somehow.

Surely the pain must have been far greater for my Mom because she had taken the harshest decision of all. She left one of my siblings in the care of an adoption center. I closed my eyes to tell myself that it was alright to fill myself with a fabricated sense of hope. At least, this way, one of my siblings would have a safe place to live until Mom would come back to get them. Tears, numbness, and a slapping reality was what I felt in that one moment when we were to walk away from our sibling. I cannot even fathom what my sibling must have endured? Not one of us wished to be apart from the other, even for a day. But life was cruel. It gave us no leniency.

By now, God should have shown mercy to us. We were going through a drought of annihilation. But things only grew worse for us. The withering hope for my family worsened, and my Mom had to leave yet another one of my siblings in the adoption center. She had no more money, and our journey was far from its beginning. By now, I knew fear, worry, eagerness, and hazard better than the back of my hand. However, pushing all of this aside, faith was still flickering within me. Even if it was just a glim, it was enough to keep my body from going cold. With a heavy heart, my Mom finally managed to put up enough money for us to fly to an island on San Andrea next - an island that waited for us with open arms but full of thorns. Every thorn offered us different suffering. Each one of that thorn pricked deep within our skin, inflicting a new challenge on us to overcome each time.

Recalling those memories crush my heart, and to look back at it all, I am truly awed how my family and I surpassed all odds. When we reached San Andreas, a literal storm awaited us and was only gaining more strength, due to which the island we were on was nearly vacant. All of the piling stress finally started to take a toll on my Mom's health. In a time where she was to be at complete bed rest, her feet were developing blisters. When she was to replenish herself with nutrient-rich food, she was scampering for a morsel. And the one to pay the price was the baby in her womb.

Mom started to show signs of complications, her face paling, and her body unable to carry her weight anymore. She still tried to push herself to be with us, to keep us under the wings of her protection. They say if you truly wish to achieve something, never give up, and so she did. But instead of relishing in the rewards of it, she only collapsed. This was the point when she finally had to face another gruesome challenge – she left us in the care of Susana and took my brother with Richard to Honduras to have the baby.

Before leaving, I remember Mom looking in our eyes, silently begging us for forgiveness but staking a vow, *"Don't worry, my girls, you are strong. Mommy knows you are; after all, you are my little princesses. I will be back soon, till then you be good to Susana."*

"Yes, Mommy. We love you." That was all we said before our Mom disappeared from our sight.

She left and never once turned back. But I did not whimper. I knew I had to be strong now. Even though I was just a child like my siblings, I knew I had to keep myself composed for their sake. I reprimanded myself for mourning over my loss any longer, as I had to be the one to keep us all together – safe and sound.

Mom was to come shortly after having the baby. She had left us with enough money to stay in the hotel till then. In her absence, suddenly, each hour became prominent. Each tick of the clock was blaring to us, and the days seemed longer. Waiting became miserable for us, and we started to wonder if she would ever come back for us. Susana was no great help either. It was only my sisters and me, looking after one another.

Then, one day, we heard from our Mom. She contacted us to let us know that she was sending enough money for all of us to travel to Honduras, as she would not be coming back. Back then, she had never shared the reason why it took her so long, and we only discovered it later. We were elevated, nonetheless, because we were going back to her. We were prepared and could not help chatting amongst ourselves. My sisters argued who would get to hug Mom first, and we patiently waited for Susana to return to the hotel room. She had left claiming to collect the money Mom had sent for us and get bus tickets so we could leave immediately. But our wait never seemed to come to an end. Hours passed by. Dawn turned to dusk. The air outside grew stale from its previous humidity, but Susana never came back.

"Where is Susana, Rosa?" My sister asked, looking frightened.

I turned to look at the faces of all my sisters, who were shielding their frames by placing their hands against their chests

Chapter 4
The Struggle

My sisters' eyes bore into mine, silently praying for a miracle. It crippled me to see them terrified. We were all aware of the night-howls of this part of the world. It was no safer than our previous residence at the hotel in Medellin. I kept glancing at my sisters, my mind racing fast in the hopes of securing a solution, but none came. There was no way for us to contact Susana. Part of us worried about her well-being, and part of us pondered if she betrayed us. No answer came, and we sat huddled together, praying to God to help us out. Alas, no help came.

My sisters kept questioning Susana's whereabouts, but I was not equipped with an answer. She had left telling us all that she would be back, but the sky was threatening to turn dark now. It petrified me, just as much as it troubled my sisters. We were alone, and the people surrounding us were aware of it. We were innocent prey for predators lurking around us. Each knock in the hallway of the hotel and each creaking footstep sent shivers up and down our spines. I could feel my heart sinking. By now, I was certain that

Susana would not return.

"Rosa..." my sister croaked before she broke down, bawling her eyes out.

I wanted to pacify my sister. When I attempted to wrap my arms around her and tried to calm her down, I failed to believe my own words. Susana had betrayed us. She never came back for us and had fled with all the money. We were left completely crippled, mentally, and financially. My thoughts were running wild with the possibilities of getting help. I could not have gone knocking at the doors of a stranger. It would only have jeopardized our lives even more. So what were my options? I tried to remember our way to the hotel. Luckily, I recalled a white-house type embassy near our hotel. I faced my sisters, my eyes gleaming with hope. I held my sister's hand, reassuringly.

"I need you to lock the door and go hide under the bed. Do not open until I come back, not even for Susana, ok?"

"Where are you going?" They asked. Their faces were still dull as they clung to my hand tightly.

"I am going to get help."

"No! Don't go. Don't leave us, Rosa." They begged me, and I felt as if someone had stabbed my heart.

"We don't have a choice. I promise I will return. Until then, lock the door carefully, and if possible, place a piece of furniture against it and hide under the bed. Ok?" I said, looking at them.

They exchanged glances before nodding at me. Then we embraced one another tightly. I promised myself that no matter what was to come, I would never abandon them. Exchanging our goodbyes, I managed to storm past the staircase and out in the streets alone. I had never been out in this city before. I felt scared. I was just a child who needed protection. My sisters and I were not supposed to be stranded like this. We were not supposed to be separated from our parents. Most importantly, we were not supposed to be fending for ourselves, to be running like this on a perilous street.

Outside, I could feel each pair of eyes bore into my skin while I was running blindly, yet I did not stop. I knew if I stopped, I would be swallowed whole by the evil surrounding us. So even when my skin burned and my legs begged me to stop, even when my lungs parched and my throat craved a drop of water to quench my thirst, I ran. I only stopped when a big white building came before me. I stopped in front of it and made my way up the steps to an office. My body seemed to have registered that I was safe now.

Voices came from the room in front, so I went inside until grim faces came into my view. As soon as I entered the room, silence draped all over the room. It felt as if they had seen a ghost. An office that was a moment ago lively was now absolutely quiet. Concerned laced the eyes of men there, and furrows dented across their forehead. With a tremoring voice, I managed to push all doubts aside and confide in them.

"My sisters and I are alone."

These words seemed to have bewildered them. Instantly, a bunch of them rushed to me, and I cried. I finally cried. After weeks, my emotions became far too much for me to hold within myself. I quivered as I told them everything, from my Mom bringing us to Columbia through Peru to her going to Honduras to have her baby. I told them how the very person who was sworn to keep us safe ran at the first opportunity that came her way. I told them that we were alone and scared. I told them we had no one and just wanted to go back home.

I was tended to immediately. An older woman tried to comfort me. But the more she tried, the more I cried. My situation was finally clear to me. My sisters and I were in trouble. We had no clue where our Mom was and had no means to contact them. Soon enough, the place rendered me help. From helicopters to motorcycles, all form of help was dispatched as I went with them to rescue my sisters. Finally, seeing my sisters out of the hotel room filled me with gratitude and relief.

My sisters ran to me as we hugged one another, holding hands tight before we were ushered to a police station. The situation there, however, was far different than I could have expected. Men and women dressed in uniforms looked at us pitifully. The words they exchanged only riled me. Their words were adorned with a distaste for my Mom. It angered me the more they spoke among themselves. I was sitting on a bench in the police station, while these people freely labeled my mother irresponsible. They said my mother was a terrible woman who could not care for her children. The people of authority conversed with ease, never once considering the turmoil their words were making me go through.

"SHE IS NOT TERRIBLE!" I yelled, standing up suddenly. Silence prevailed as they were all stunned now. My sisters tried to pull me back, evidently frightened by these people. They told me to sit down, but I only yelled more. Tears welled up in my swollen eyes, and they burnt. *"My Mom is not terrible! She is trying to get us! She sent money, but Susana ran away with it! Our Mommy loves us. You don't know her."*

My voice turned hysteric, triggering my sisters to mourn with me. It seemed we were alone. Some of the faces were laden with guilt, and some were vexed. That night I was shown how I was the adult of my family now. I had to be the one to keep all of us together; else, people would only cripple us beneath their shoes. The police alerted the necessary authorities and the embassy. Later, they told me that my sisters and I were to be separated for the time being. Crying was all that we knew. But even as we wailed and begged, the decision was taken on our behalf.

Thoughts of never uniting with my family prevailed. My sisters disappeared from my vision as they were sent along with the President Secretary's Mom. Meanwhile, I was placed in the care of the ambassador I had approached, only to begin a life of further misery. One would think these people living in the luxury of velvet bedding and silken linen would be at least compassionate toward a child, but the truth is, they were not. No one came to check on us or tell us if we were ever to be returned to our family.

My presence was nothing but a blessing for the ambassador, as she instantly hired me as child labor. I knew I was at her mercy, and if I disobeyed her commands, I might never get a chance to be with my sisters. So, I bowed my head to her orders. From waking up daily at 4 a.m. to wash her clothes, feed the chicken, and selling coffee to cooking and cleaning her entire house till late at night, I was to work and work without ever complaining. Days, I would scold myself for having sought their help, and nights, I would cry myself to sleep, missing my family. I would fall asleep praying for the safety of my siblings and Mom.

No information was shared if the authorities had contacted our Mom or managed to find Susana. I was starting to believe that this was my life now. The only thread of hope still holding me intact was how this experience was teaching me to be self-reliant. After two months of being alone, the ambassador commanded me to sit in a car. She drove me back to the very place where it all had begun. I was beginning to wonder if she was finally letting me go. Maybe she did not want a burden on her, but a surprise awaited me. I entered the police station.

"*ROSA!*" their voices led me to turn on my heels.

The biggest grin came on my lips with tears lacing my eyes. I ran toward my sisters, as they ran in my direction and we encompassed one another in bliss. I felt alive after fighting a long battle of loneliness. This time I was adamant about not parting ways with my sister, even if it meant to escape the very people I sought. Thankfully, this time we were not separated. The decision for someone to take us with them was not the optimal solution. I was glad whoever made this decision had a heart.

My sisters and I were left to relive the times when we had first come here and sat on the benches observing the people. They were running around, yelling amidst themselves what to do next. They were unable to reach Mom and beginning to conclude that she had abandoned us. No solution came forth. They were unable to trace the whereabouts of our parents. I turned to look at my sisters. Their thoughts were just as distorted as mine. We failed to recall the last time we had a decent meal or the last time we slept in peace? Nightmares were a usual occurrence now when I would wake up gasping for air. At times, I would envision my Daddy committing suicide, and at times, I would see myself never meeting with my family again. My eyes were fixated on each figure before me as they came to a standstill. It was then declared that we were traveling back to Bogota - the place that initiated our misfortune.

Once we reached Bogota, I was beginning to think maybe they would send us back to Peru, to our Dad. Instead, we were recklessly discarded in one of the worst adoption centers there. The conditions there were so gruesome and horrid that children were treated worse than pests. The only consolation that kept me buoyant was the company of my sisters. At least we were together, and this way, I was able to care for them better.

At the adoption center, I must say that I had the fortune of meeting with some of the most amazing souls. It was astonishing, nerve-racking, and heartbreaking to see so many innocent souls with no one to care for them. The children there had a sense of relentless willpower to hope for better days. Even when they were given all the reasons to believe that life was not for them, they had managed to construct a sanctuary of their own.

My sisters and I were welcomed with open arms to a community of infinite dreams, purest of smiles, and the bravest of souls. I met the youngest mother in the world – a nine-year-old girl who was pregnant. I saw children who were raped by the very protectors of the adoption center. It was ironic, how a place established to take care of these children and provide them with another opportunity in life treated them like rags.

Aren't children like flowers? Aren't they the budding future of this world? Then why were they treated as if they had no soul? Each day there filled me with concern for my sisters. I knew I had to protect them from the lecherous eyes of all those around us. It was hard to live in such an environment, but the only thing that kept me afloat was the children around me. Seeing them fighting each day after repeatedly getting violated was my only beacon of hope. I knew I had to get out of that place. It was a dungeon where we were captives. Had I not tried to fight the system, they would have separated my sisters from me permanently. People still came to the adoption center to pick children under the pretext of providing them with a family. But it was untrue. Knowing I had to do something, one day when the guard was not around, I opened a small window. It was enough for me to escape and be on the run once more. So, I crept out the window and sought help from the Peruvian embassy.

Out of all the troubles laid for us, the Peruvian embassy turned out to be my only consolation. Unlike the other embassy we had gone to, this one was swift to take strict measures. My sisters and I were once more rescued and placed in an adoption center far better than the previous one with the promise of finding our Mom. Alas, if our Mom was to take long, then the condition for us being adopted separately still dangled above her head like a sword. We still had not heard a word from our Mom. I had a little reason to believe that she would be coming back for us. There was little for me to trust, except for memories. They were my life jacket amidst the turmoil. At the adoption center, I soon befriended other children as I happened to be the eldest among them. It was a gift I received in the form of trust all these children placed in me. I became an elder sister to all of them, as they had watched me tend to my sisters. I soon developed a sacred bond with these children who shared a story similar to mine, with a few different hues of life. But it was the only thing we had in common – of lost family. Despite some of the children being unwanted and some having lost their parents, they continued to smile each day. It was a miracle to see them smile when they had all the reasons to cry. How were they so strong? They reminded me of the stars, shining brighter in a night sky.

Like stars, they shone, but if you were to take a closer look, you could see their scars depicting their nightmares. Some of the children had fended for themselves for far too long by living on the streets. Some of them were raped. It broke my heart each time one of them spoke to me. What inspired me was that they did not allow their past to define their future. It was inspiring to see them brimming with courage. They were truly brave to stand tall each day. They were grateful for getting a chance to breathe and wake up each morning. They made sure never to be ungrateful by always smiling.

These children gave me hope, and I started to believe that my mother would come too. She was not the one to abandon us. I thought she would come one day like a miracle. Meeting the children over there - the trapped souls - turned out to be the key to unlock my belief and faith. I then picked out another sacred memory from the library of memoirs in my mind to share with them. I shared with them my memory of seeing God, and we all agreed that God is there.

We cannot run from our destiny. We cannot comprehend the plans of God. We are only to hope that better days lie ahead of us, and it is every bit true. The children became my source of comfort, as I became theirs. They aided me in persevering and being resilient. They revived my hope that Mommy would come, as I exchanged it for a promise that the day Mom would come, we would come back for them, and I would free them all. I was naïve back then to have made such a big promise, but it did fill them with hope. I gave them something to live for.

However, my hope prevailed. Four months later, as Christmas came, it brought me my Christmas miracle. A day forever engraved in my brain. Just like the moment at the bus stop in Peru when I had seen my Dad, I relived that very moment all over again, except this time, it was Mom. I stood shocked with tears welling up in my eyes. She was here. My sisters and I ran like the wind, untamed, and crashed in her embrace as she hugged back with just as much might.

"My babies," she said.

I never wanted to let go of my Mom again. I was afraid if I were to remove my arms from around her, she would slip away. I did not want that. Consoling ourselves as reality settled that she was actually her, we finally broke our embrace.

"My babies. I am so sorry. Mommy wanted to come earlier, but they did not let me. I am so sorry, my babies."

I could not help but question *"Who?"* Why was someone stopping our Mom from meeting us?

"The authorities. They did not let me come to you. But now, I am here. I fought them. I fought with all of the authorities. They were about to let you all up for adoption. They cannot keep my babies away from me. Come on now, let's go."

As promised, our Mom did not leave us there for even a second. She held our hands in hers, and we walked out with her.

"Mom, do we have a brother or sister now?" I asked innocently.

With all worries gone from my mind, I started to wonder who my new sibling was. But instead of getting an answer, my Mom looked down at her feet as we stopped.

"The baby?" She asked. I nodded in response. She inhaled deeply before bending on her knees and cupping my face, *"The baby is no more, Rosa."* Perturbed, my eyes squinted. *"Rosa, this is why I couldn't come. I had complications, because of which the baby died."*

"Mom…" I tried to speak, but she tugged our hands, ushering us to go.

With a heavy heart, we walked away. Our heads hung low as our minds started to grasp all the events within the past months. It was truly devastating how we faced one loss after another. But time was not done playing tricks on us. Our woes were nowhere near the end. As we walked to the bus stop, we passed by a newspaper stand. That was where my eyes caught the sight of a photo in the newspaper. It was our photo printed in the newspaper. And not just one but many.

It seemed the Peruvian embassy had alerted our Dad too, and he was trying to look for us. But before he could have reached us, our Mom came, and once more, we took the next bus out of Bogota with a baggage full of uncertainties.

Chapter 5
Running Away

They say, after a hurricane comes a rainbow, but it seemed the rainbow that was to shed color on our lives was hidden away. The skies for us were dark, looming with so many perils we could never have imagined in our wildest dreams. Hunger was the least of our worries as we watched our mother trying to cower us away from the sight of all those around us. Yes, we were that famous in Bogota. The credit for it goes to my father, who was trying to come to our rescue, unbeknown that our mother had already retrieved us from the horrifying conditions of the adoption center.

We witnessed it firsthand. I remember seeing mine and my siblings' faces plastered on all publications – newspaper, magazines, flyers, adorning every rack and shelf of every single newspaper stand in the city. Be it at a station, on the road, or tucked away in an alley, our faces were painted everywhere. It triggered a flickering ray of hope within me. Maybe if my father were to find us, he would take us all back home with him. Me, my Mom, my siblings, and my father, and then maybe we could be that complete family finally.

Yes, I still longed for this. I was tired of this chase but did not want to leave my mother. I knew she was trying so hard to keep us together and safe from all harm. However, nothing seemed to have worked in her favor yet. She was frightened that the father would take us back to Peru, so she made us hop onto the first bus that she saw. It was only the beginning of another tiresome journey. We were drenched in sweat and hardship. It seemed we were stranded in a tunnel that was not coming to an end. Despite knowing there was meant to be a light at the other end, the more we tried to reach toward it, the more it grew out of our reach.

My siblings and I would see people eating food around, and our stomachs would growl. But we repressed this. We held back our starvation. We had to, as we had no other choice because we knew our mother had no money. The only hope we had at that time that helped me the most to hang on was my brother and Richard back in Honduras. The bus was just taking us away from the adoption center. We had embarked on a journey from city to city in the hopes of finding kindness. Let me tell you; kindness was scarce to find back then. People did not want to stop for a second and hear the plight of another soul. They would shrug off and walk. I walked in the shadows of my mother until we reached Barranquilla. It happened to be rather close to the borders of Panama and Columbia, adding on to the frenzied state of the place a shade of doubt. The place was far peculiar than I can state in words.

What was amazing as well as perplexing was that we were complete strangers there. My mother knew not a single soul. We were all that we knew. Together we walked the streets of this new place under the scorching sun in the hopes of basking in the coolness of help. Bit by bit as much as I did my best to hide my state, watching my mother helpless and my siblings suffer, I was going crazy. I only hid my emotions as best I could as a child. No one took mercy on us. People we ran into and asked for help turned us down. It was a rejection that inched us closer to fall apart. I fail to understand how my mother managed to keep her composure, how she kept herself together, and us safe from further harm.

In a world that was unsafe for women, my mother walked the streets with her daughters alone, with her head held high, dignified, and secure. We had no money, nothing on us but our dignity, and she guarded it with all her might. The city of Barranquilla was no less uncharitable to us until we came across this old soul. At first sight, the man was very inviting and humble. He was just a local barber who lived above his modest shop. Slowly as his first layer peeled off, I realized he was no less nasty and vile as any other man. Still, he was our only hope. As they say that beggars cannot be choosy, so we stayed mum.

The old man offered us his place to stay. By his place, I mean the cold concrete floor swarmed by cockroaches that induced nightmares. The offer was enticing to us nonetheless. It was better that we slept with a roof above our head than letting the sky cloak us with unknown hazards that come to life after midnight. Hence, as much as I had the feeling of a critter crawling beneath my skin, gripping me tightly, and chills running up and down my spine, I would hurdle closer to my sisters and try to think of a lullaby that would differ with the cruelty we were engulfed in.

The cackle of men would erupt from beneath the shop. Each time a man would laugh, we were able to feel wickedness lacing their voice as the barber would tell them about us, and it would rouse an eerie emotion within us. We knew something was not quite right. Back then, I could never have thought of what was going on. The help discarded our way was nothing but a pretext to lure us into something far gruesome. For the few nights we stayed there, each night, the barber or one of his patrons would invite my mother to go upstairs alone. I did not want my mother to leave us for a split second. But this man was the one to have placed a roof above our head, and I knew it would be hard for her to say no. But I was just a child. I did not know how strong she truly was. She would deal with the old man in such a way that it would extend our stay for a day more. After a couple of days, it became hard for her to stay there as the old man was posing a threat, not only to her but also to us. So, we left. We left the cockroach-infested shop, hoping to find another shelter soon.

Hope is such an amazing feeling in this world. It gives a person a purpose when they have nothing. Hope hands a person an invisible thread to hold on, and it works like the charm of a strong rope fastened around that person to prevent them from falling. It was the same for us. Even when we had nothing, and we could no longer carry our own burden, we continued fighting this invisible force that was against us, irrespective of how people still turned us down. Not one person would stop to assist us. We still continued to walk until our mother took us to a local Catholic church.

Growing up, my mother would take my siblings and me to our local Catholic church often. It was the kind of sanctuary where everyone knew everyone in Latin America. What was even more surprising was that all the priests there were Jewish converts. No one ever felt out of place, as we were all the children of God coming together to pray in unison. Thus, when I entered this church, I expected the same sentiment of belongingness to embrace me. But it never did. While the atmosphere was not hostile, unlike the streets, the priest did render us a listening ear. My mother confided in him and poured her heart out.

After surviving the harsh behavior of the people and the ruthlessness of the cities, the priest provided us with our first decent meal in weeks. We were quick to gobble each morsel down, not knowing when we would be getting our next meal. The priest even provided my mother with a beer. It was somewhat a tradition in Columbia, where the drink would be offered to let the guest be at ease. My thankful mother drank the beer, and my siblings looked rested— the calmness of the church sprawled over us like a comforter in a biting January night. I never wanted to let it go. I wanted to clutch on to this tighter and construct a shelter for my family. So, I hoped or may have thought the priest would provide us with help. He would provide us with a roof or money to help us evade this city and reach out to my brother.

The outcome, however, was not the same. We left. We left the church as well. We were turned down by the church as well. All that we were granted was a moment of peace and silence, along with a decent meal and a beer for my mother to re-energize herself. The moment I thought we would be happy again was the moment we were shown devastation. The priest did not help us in any way, and we were left to fend for ourselves. We were back on the streets, our silhouettes standing alone in a crowd. It seemed we were a plague when it came to seeking help, but when it came to the lecherous gazes of men, we were the only ones then.

Another wind of suffering came our way as we were back on the streets. This time we even slept on the pavement, exposed and vulnerable to the cruelty of streets. For days, my mother would take us with her. Like resilient soldiers, we marched along. Our life was a battlefield of survival, after all. This continued for days. I looked forward to daylight. It made me feel better and gave me hope that we might stumble across our rickety luck.bMy hope came true. After a few more days living on the streets as if our lives did not matter, my mother came across a marine guy. He seemed keen to listen to us. He listened intently to our dilemma, and it seemed he was affected by it. He told us not to worry, and for a moment, we took a breath. We paused. He provided us with an address.

The marine guide told us to go to the address, which was of his boss, the person in-charge of the Marine base. The man guided us to the base and told us to seek shelter there, for someone would surely be willing to help us. By now, we were desperate and did as we were told. Never once did any doubt cross our minds. We trusted the person and went over to the address for our next tribulation to commence. He had told us that we would be taken care of, which was partially true.

It seems in this society a woman alone is only viewed as a bodily gain; she is not thought of as a human too. You would think that an educated person would think differently, but no. If a woman is alone, men will think of taking advantage of her. But, certainly not all men. I can vouch for this as there were genuine angels who came our way, but most of the men my mother came across, they were willing to help her in turn of something illicit. Once we reached the marine base, we were taken in immediately and offered sustenance. But as night began to crawl in, a different scene started to unfold. What I saw over there was a whole new definition of crazy.

At night, the downstairs of the base would turn into a dark world that promised prostitution and drugs. The marine guys would flood the place after dinner to indulge in promiscuous sex. They would party hard every night. There is no subtle way to put in words what I saw there. Among all the marines who were staying there, my mother was the only woman.

Well, not the only one exactly, as there was another woman amidst the sea of men who happened to be the wife of one of the marine men. That woman was living there with her son, who happened to be a year older than me. My mother must have thought if another woman was living, then surely it must not be that bad. Also, we were getting a free meal and were not on the roads, so we settled there for a while. By then, I was well-versed with what darkness is and what isolation is. I was home-sick. I missed my father, our house, and the life we had before everything turned upside down. My family was wrecked, and it crippled my heart. I would have done anything to put things in order, but I guess the universe was the one in control. For days, we stayed at the base and hoped to stay far from danger for as long as possible. During our stay there, I witnessed a day that haunts me to date. It is etched in my memory. I can never get rid of it, no matter how hard I try.

I was changing in the room upstairs, and like any door, there was a peephole in it. Well, it was just a key-opening but a peephole for others. Oblivious to how corrupt a person can be, I was changing when an unknown emotion started to crawl against my skin. I could feel an unnamed sensation on my skin. There was someone present in the room with me. I froze, and so did time. Slowly, I turned on my heels; my eyes were ransacking the room for an intrusive presence. I could feel lingering against my exposed skin. That boy, the son of the marine wife, was the unsolicited audience.

Tears welled up in my eyes, and I scurried to grab my clothes and veil my chastity as quickly as possible. At the same time, the boy scrambled away. Seeing me frantic, he realized that I had realized he was intruding in on my privacy. Each second disgusted me. I was paralyzed after having covered myself. This, however, was not the end of it. Many incidents similar in nature took place throughout our stay there. The people were taking advantage of our helpless state, and we had no means of defense. One of the reasons why the person in-charge of the base had allowed us to stay in the first place was my mother. He had developed an impure interest in her. All he wanted was to spend a night with her. We were defenseless against so many people sharing the same intention.

Thankfully, our luck shone on us. The rays of safety reached us in the form of Eduardo. Amidst a sea of people who were wolves in sheep's clothing was a true angel who came forth at the right time. He was one of the marine guys who truly wanted to help us. He helped us flee the marine base and took us to a gigantic boat. The ship seemed larger than the Titanic. Of course, the ship was not for cruising purposes.

The ship seemed to be a petroleum or oil carrier. Eduardo helped us get on that ship. He came along with us as well. This ship became our very first haven. After months of being on the run, after weeks of torture and misery, we came to a resting place. Unsure where the ship was heading, we got on it knowing he was with us. We stepped on this buoyant city that promised to take us afar from everything. We were offered a room to ourselves, a kitchen, food, and clothing. All expenses were taken care of generously by him. Why was he doing this? Why was he kind to us when people only wanted to tarnish us?

As much as we did not want to know the truth, for we feared Eduardo would turn out to be selfish as well, we came across a revelation that left us stunned. We had been on the ship for nearly a month. For a month, we trusted him blindly and became friends with him. He got us everything we needed and took great care of us. We were showered with his relentless care. He treated us as his own. The reason for it was that he had started to think of us as his. While we developed a deeper bond with him, he considered us as his own children because he had fallen in love with my mother. Let's take a deep breath here. This man who was helping us to no ends had fallen in love with my mother. How can this be? When everyone else was attracted to my mother, Eduardo saw her for the woman she truly was - courageous, fierce, strong, and tender. She was everything a man could dream of, a partner who did not rely on anyone but herself.

So, he fell in love with her. By then, we had discovered that she had started to like him as well. Truth be told, how can she not have taken a liking to a man as selfless as him? He was kind and never crossed his line. He never tried to take advantage of her but treated us better than Richard.

This was a new crossroads for us. Eduardo was willing to accept my mother for who she was and us as well. He wanted to make her a part of his life. He wanted to shelter her and us from all of the storms. He was offering us a life of peace and sanity. What an enticing offer after we had undergone tremendous afflictions.

But, there was a hindrance. She was still in love with Richard, and she still had to rescue our brother, Hosier, who was in an adoption center in Honduras. We had to go back to Honduras to Richard and my brother. We had to go back and get my brother. Sadly, this life Eduardo was creating for us was temporary, just like the voyage we were on. My mother managed to muster the courage and put aside this new feeling she was brewing. Once more, she had to confess how she had a lover waiting for her, and she was trying to get back to him. She told Eduardo this was not our journey, and being the altruistic person he was, he understood.

Instead of forcing himself like a nasty person, he stepped aside. A month and a half of knowing him, the time came when we had to take our leave. We had to bid our goodbye. But this was not all to the love and care he had showered on us. Being aware of our predicament and not finding any sort of profit for him in all of this, he did one last deed that I can never forget or repay. Before he disappeared from our lives for good, he gave my mother money.

Eduardo was aware that we would need money to continue our journey. He knew that my mother had no source of income or family to count on. So as we started to tread a new road, it was filled with the shelter of Eduardo's care for us. The time we spent with him was no less than a vacation. It was enough to fill our mind and body with new-found strength. With this courage, with this flaring will to find our happiness and a way out, we continued to cross cities after cities. Jumping from one boat to another for days, our only vision was of the folding waves. At times an inviting blue, and at times an enticing shade of aqua, we crossed waters in boats, we skimmed through rivers in canoes, and then we traced the curves of highways in buses.

Our journey was filled with ups and downs. From the swaying motion of the sea to the bumping of roads, my shoulder was a pillow for my siblings, and the light snores of the passengers around us were my lullabies. My mother continued to walk until we reached a little town by this virgin jungle that generously adorned the borders of Panama and Columbia. (Unable to understand the name of the jungle in the recording). It was the kind of jungle that left passersby intrigued. From the giant trees with their roots gnawed deep within the grounds to the soft whispering bugs and creatures living in, it was a sight that left my mother and others around us bewildered, including me.

I was fascinated by this jungle. While I overheard my mother having conversed with others how no one ever trod this jungle, or at least it was the word of the town, I wanted to know what lived deep within it. I was pulled to the jungle. My mother was worried that if she had to cross it, how would she do so? She was not alone. She had the responsibility of my siblings and me. We were unaware of the residents of the jungle. The jungle was painted all the more mysterious with the spoken words around us. The entire ordeal was no less than a scene from a movie of an invitation to an adventure of a lifetime. I wanted to experience it. It seemed my unspoken wish was about to come true. My family and I made a stop in the town near the jungle, and my mother started to mingle with others in search of a new way out. Much to our astonishment, the people there were different. They were far from what we saw. This made me understand that looks are truly deceiving. From the run-down housing to men and women looking contemptible, initially, we were intimidated by them. On the other hand, as my mother spoke with them, their voice was filled with awe and sympathy.

These very people I deemed to be unreliable turned out to be the opposite. They listened to us and marveled at our journey - a journey of a woman alone with her daughters, separated only to be united. Now we were on a quest to be united with our brother before we could go to a land that seemed far away. Nonetheless, it was all worth it, or so we had conceived. After acknowledging how we were truly in need of aid, these people promised my mother with a passage, but there was a constraint. Apparently, there was an infamous figure who could have assisted us, and at that point, we were unaware of its identity.

The people we met were fierce yet gentle. They seemed hard as wax but melted soft, just the same. They took my mother and us to their housing, and we were treated with the utmost respect. They felt like a family while they were only strangers. After months of having experienced queerness, I finally felt that I was at home. No threat lingered around me. We were greeted with smiling faces and generous hearts. We had a meal to share with these people who soon started to consider us one of their own.

Our stay there soon started to come to an end. After all, we were not there to mingle with them, but meet this man they did not stop swooning about. These people who invited us to live with them were working for this mysterious man. We were clueless about what to expect, and so we walked with these people to meet this man whom everyone was continuously singing praises of.

After my mother had agreed to go with them, these people finally revealed the identity of the person – Pablo Escobar. Back then, I had never heard of this name. I had no idea that he was the man who was responsible for the disheveled state of Medellin. So when I overheard my mother finding out and her being weary, I was confused. I remember the words vividly – would it be safe for my daughters and me to meet the man who ran the mafia? I recalled Richard's comment then, of a mafia being responsible for the shrieks and the plight of people, and the scarlet tainting all streets of Medellin. Blood was everywhere. When my family would go out to eat or change our accommodation when we were in Medellin, we would only come across one sight – crimson red of humanity discarded on the ground.

Nevertheless, we were assured if there was one person who would be able to help us, it was Pablo Escobar. How was it possible, though? A man who orders for the mass assassination was to help a family like ours? At the same time, we were living with his men.

These people, who lived a life of normalcy and who were not rich but lived comfortably with all that they needed, were happy to be employed by him. In a short time that we were there, we got to know of their families, their wives, and girlfriends. Music would be playing all around, and people would be truly merry. Even the wives and girlfriends of these men lived in harmony. These very people shared with us that if a man was working for the mafia, they were considered to be among the luckiest. So working for Pablo Escobar was truly an honor. They shared with us how they owed their cheerful livelihood to him. Living amongst them, no one could have suspected these men were assassins and smugglers. They were passionate and kind. They shared the other side to Mr. Escobar, one which was not notorious. It was a side to him that was charitable of him helping those in need of assistance. Surely, there was a cost to it during days when he felt charitable. In return for helping people cross the border, he would basically use these people as transportation for information or drugs.

Understanding everything, my mother agreed to let them introduce us to Pablo Escobar. We were told that we would be taking a long, long walk in order to meet him. His bodyguards shared that Mr. Escobar had gone to pay his daughter a visit, who was living in a hideout. Soon enough, it was revealed that the house he was living in happened to be situated away from the virgin jungle. We had to cross it in order to meet him. The moment was filled with dread. My mother had to make a decision. We could either fend on the streets and suffer or make this journey in the hopes of finding salvation. Not having much to lose and having observed how these people treated us, my mother agreed, and we began trekking the jungle. We cut across lush greenery, filling our vision, as soil tainted our soles. The sky was only visible from the creaks of the canopy of towering trees. We continued to walk after these bodyguards to meet an affluent man who would possibly help us. My thoughts were a mix of excitement and uncertainty. It seemed Mr. Escobar was our last hope.

When we arrived at the house after hours' worth of walk, my first thought was that we were fooled. There was no establishment in sight except for trees that were already inhabiting the jungle. There were trees everywhere, hills green with envy for not having a voice, and a sparkling stream along the side. It was an oasis. Turning on our heels, we came to know that it was indeed an oasis of Mr. Escobar.

Veiled by the trees was his mansion, where his daughter resided. We walked past the trees to see a new crowd flooding the place. From not seeing a single soul, my vision was filled with people walking in and out, like a busy street of a business hub. For a moment, I thought we were meeting with a minister, and then it hit me that he was no less than that for the people who worked for him. I gulped down the lump in my throat full of worry and walked behind my family in silence. We had no clue what to expect. The house was just as brilliant and amazing as the landscape. It was surrounded by guards. People were crossing them to get to him. With us were a girl and an old woman, who we later discovered was Mr. Escobar's mother. The young girl was his daughter. As excited as I was, I turned around to watch my mother's jittering teeth. She was taken aback by the happenings and was trembling. I had never seen her as perturbed as she was. The next thing I knew was that we were being approached by Mr. Escobar himself. Each step he took toward us roused tension in our bodies.

Finally, he came to stand before us. He looked like an ordinary Joe - a tall person with a beer belly and thick black hair. No one could have assumed this man was running a mafia. In a gentle voice, he asked if my mother would care for a drink. This was it. A simple Colombian tradition of offering drinks to the guest was all that it took to ease my mother. Her nervousness ceased. This was the beginning of a new passage for us. Looking back at the new adventure we were about to step foot on; my mother had portrayed exemplary courage. Now it is not easy to meet someone of great affluence, let alone a carter who is renowned worldwide for his brutality and acclaimed for his charitable side. There my mother stood, having walked into his territory with her children, asking for help. What she had done back then was worthy of applause. We were not disappointed. Life was turning gentle toward us for once. There was a possibility that she would not have to endure another battle for rescuing my brother alone, as we hoped for Mr. Escobar to assist us with the task. That was what I had in my mind back then.

The change of fate was more than what I expected. We were welcomed into Mr. Escobar's residence with open arms. I got to know his daughter, his mother, him as a person, and all the people who worked for him. We were treated like queens and served with delicious meals, including my favorite beverage, Apple Postobon, a soda I loved. Even now, I love that soda. It always refreshes my memory of the day I had it there. My family was not there alone. There were other children too; all of them were treated with respect. Mr. Escobar had ordered food for us, and we were being served.

All the people there were catered to as per his orders. After a long time, I felt at ease and safe. I felt as safe as I felt within my own home. The only thing that lacked was the feeling of being home. I knew I was under observation, but I accepted it. This was far better than all that I had to withstand to reach this place. Being there, my mother had gone to converse with Mr. Escobar. From the corner of my eyes, I observed it all; how she would be forced to pause every five minutes as people would come in and out. The place was buzzing with a different energy, and Mr. Escobar was tending to all of them. Even his daughter had left, but my mother was waiting patiently to relay our quandary to him. He was our last resort.

Reflecting back on all of that, it feels like a dream. An eccentric and surreal dream I lived through. The entire momentum was vast. We were meeting with a mafia king in the hopes of him helping us somehow. Much true to his words, Mr. Escobar, after having paid attention to our struggle, willed an offer to my mother, a simple passage to reach Honduras. The ticket was rather affordable for my mother. She was to carry a piece of information on his behalf to Honduras, where Richard and my brother were. The travel was promised by Mr. Escobar and came with a rewarding recompense.

The time for farewell was finally upon us. I had only stayed there for a few weeks, but in those weeks, I discovered something unusual. I got to see the truth of so many people. People are not always what they seem. Those who appear to be civil can be monsters. Those whom the world deems to be a monster may have an alternative reality to them. While this does not justify the act of savagery, I guess life showed me to expect all possibilities. Only in a few instances did I see Mr. Escobar raging in anger and rolling out commands that were inhumane.

I got a glimpse into different realms within one world. After we left his abode, we never saw or heard from him again. My mother, I, and my siblings all changed our last goodbyes with Mr. Escobar and his world. We left with a lighter heart and an anticipating soul that was buzzing with excitement that I would finally be seeing my brother. We left with enough money that was meant to help us cross borders until we would reach Honduras.

Chapter 6
El Tapon Del Darien

Being equipped with money, I had thought this was the end of our trials. I assumed my mother would be at ease. At the back of my mind, I was aware that our journey would be long, but little did I know that it would be excruciating as well. Before I begin this chapter, I would like to share how I doubted everything and was even upset with God at times – why did my family and I had to suffer in this way? Why weren't our problems coming to a halt? Where was our rainbow? Instead of finding an answer immediately, I found it now.

Life comes with no instructions, rules, or guidelines. It does not even adhere to these. In life, we are always tested. Each phase is a journey we need to endure. Once one journey comes to an end, the other begins shortly after. The troubles in life come at every turn and are never pleasant, but they have the ultimate power to alter the course of life just to bring us where we are supposed to be.

My mother was elevated after being handed enough cash to get us to Honduras and then the U.S. She was only unenlightened by what awaited us in the jungle. Sadly, we had to go through the maze of endless trees, soil, dirt, and obscurity to reach new lands. To add that she was terrified would be the biggest understatement. Watching her fidget and be numb, my heart turned cynic. From my previous thoughts of a tantalizing adventure to *what if something bad happens to my mother or sisters?*, I watched my mother panic helplessly, deeming for our reality to be a harsh nightmare.

I embraced myself for the unknown, and my mother embraced a nightmare that one of us might die through this journey that required us to cut through the jungle. It was the very jungle that no one ever crossed. Literally, not one soul had walked through the jungle, let alone taken shelter within it. People were known for tracing the outline of the jungle as they would tread their way through it to get to the borders, but no one pierced through it. We were told that it would take 48 hours for a person to cross through the jungle, given they were accustomed to doing so. We were anything but accustomed to the jungle. Our only glad tidings were that we were not alone. We were accompanied by thirty-six more people, including children, adults, and two Indians. Some were trying to reach the U.S. like us, and others were weaving a way out to reach a new destination.

Accepting the jungle and filling our lungs with a fading sense of expectancy of being free, we began our journey. It was supposed to take us two days to get through - two days of trekking through every high and low of twenty-five (25) mountains, two days of elongated sustenance that soon ran out, and so did our patience.

After clinging to the rickety mountains for hours, the time finally came when we had to greet the unpredictability of the river. This was all we knew and heard of before stepping within the jungle. If we were on the right side of the river, the water was to go high. If there was no way to hide and we had to cross the river to get to the other side, we needed the water to be low and hope that it did not rain. With that in mind, my sisters, my mother, and I prayed for mercy.

When times were rough, when we felt hopelessness triumphing, my mother would start to pray. My sisters and I, along with others, would fall in her footsteps to remember God and His mercy. But why were we praying? Why were we seeking the clemency of God? The answer was the river. The spiteful and vile river we were crossing. Some of the people who were traveling with us had already fallen victim to the hungering roars of the river, and to think of crossing it meant that it might claim another life. Each time we had to cross the river, it would drive us to the brink of insanity to know that we might lose another soul. It was like we had to sacrifice one of us each time we were to cross the river. To watch a person walking with us drown all of a sudden was heart-wrenching, yet we continued to push ourselves to cross the river.

Despite all that, I was in awe of the jungle. It had left me stunned to my core. It was its puzzling mystery that intrigued me the most. I must say, it lured part of me into wanting to discover the jungle for what it truly was. I recall seeing those gigantic ants, the black, red, and brown ones that were a nightmare for all. Their beastliness was one thing that terrified me, but after watching them alive and working, I now understand what people mean by ants being hard-workers. They were no less than warriors, trooping through the forest fearlessly and carrying either fruits or leaves away. One after another, they formed a train-like structure, transporting resources. There were times when I only saw leaves moving, and I would be stunned. To me, it was nature in its play and a sight that can never be forgotten. It was like a dream. I would think to myself, *"How are these leaves walking?"* Because that was what it was. The leaves came to life, and I was awestruck.

The ants taught me an important lesson – to work hard for whatever I want to achieve. We need to show it to the universe that we are worthy of its blessings. These ants, to them, we are giants. They should have cowered away, but they did not. They stood their ground. They worked alongside us than to have admitted defeat and run away. They chose to stay because they wanted to survive. And for survival, you do not give up. Instead of hiding away, you face your problems.

Another discovery of mine was this strange fruit-like thing. At first sight, it resembled an orange, but upon closer inspection, it revealed to have a coat of needles on it. I was just a child and was pulled to its vibrant color, not to mention the low growls of my belly that was empty. Before I could have grabbed it, however, one of the Indians traveling with us reprimanded me. He told me not even to go near the fruit as it was poisonous. I was dejected. The fruit seemed scrumptious. Curiosity was getting the best of me. But you know what they say, curiosity killed the cat. So I did as told, and I avoided the thorny fruit.

The Indians traveling with us seemed like natives of the land or at least familiar with their surroundings. They would tell us what was safe to eat and what was not. I remember plucking leaves at times that we were told were safe to eat. They were not quite a delicacy, but when a human is starved, they tend not to focus on the luxuries. Another lesson that I learned in the jungle was to be grateful for the meals we ate because some people in the world do not even have anything to eat. Hunger is one of the worst things a human can feel. It is worse than being shot. It is worse than getting your heart broken.

Nature is mesmerizing in every manner. At the beginning of our trek, we were to claim a mountain that took us twenty-four (24) hours just to get to the top. Twenty-four hours! Our legs had tinged and ached. This was not the end of our hardship. We were twenty-four more hours away from touching the ground. All I wanted to do was roll down, but it was not a possibility. What added fuel to the fire was the fact that it had not rained. We were out of the water, and the tedious climb had left our throats dry. My lips were flaky, and my mouth had stopped producing saliva.

Being thirsty, my mind could have ceased working and left me hallucinating, but what the Indians told us next worked wonders. Before either one of us could have started seeing a mirage, the Indians warned us about how the human mind works. When you are told not to do something, your mind discards everything and focuses on doing that very thing – why? The Indians left me curious, and I wanted to know *why* we were not to look back while climbing the mountain like a snail with ropes fastened around our body.

I was unable to refrain from looking back while climbing. The words of the Indians triggered me. I wanted to know for myself why they would warn us against it. So, I dared to look back. Curling my hand tighter around a rock, I steadied myself. Once certain that I was secured, I slowly twisted my neck to sweep a glance of the scene behind me. My breath had hitched in my throat, and time had frozen. My eyes dropped low to gauge just how far up we were. We were in the sky. I was a part of the fleeting white clouds within this open mass of space.

The view stunned me into silence. As I was lost in marveling at the scene, one of the Indians broke the silence with a piece of disrupting news. He cleared his voice and slowly confessed the real reason we had to hike this mountain. He told us that we needed a better view of where we were at the precise moment. From there, we had to gauge a sense of better direction toward our destiny, toward an exit out of the jungle.

Rubbles of rock kept slipping from our grip, imitating how time would run out too if we were not to find a way out. On the other hand, the bust of free air, the wafting breeze that carried an earthy scent, left me mesmerized. It had been indiscernible how being children none of us fell to our deaths, but the adults did. They plunged to their demise. Within a split second, we saw these adults losing their grip on the rocks as if they had chosen to let go than endure this battle we were in. We were combating nature without any means of an armory. Instead of fighting for life, they succumbed to their end. The scenario left me concluding only one thing; it was perhaps a matter of faith. I gather if a person has sufficient faith, they tend to face all odds. If a person believes in something, then it was a reason good enough for them to give life another chance, another day to turn over a new leaf. Faith brings forth courage. We were courageous enough to cling onto the mountain for our dear life. We knew there was hope and so we did not give in to the circumstances we were in. This is one thing I owe to my mother, who used to pray a lot with us. Praying left us spiritual.

We were not among those who would lose faith easily. Praying daily, our mother taught us how to be grateful for what we had and patient enough to wait for what we asked for. She would pray with others in the jungle as well. She would huddle my siblings and me together and ask the rest if anyone wanted to partake in praying for everyone's safety, well-being, and health.

It was no less than a miracle to see people coming forth, and we would all pray for God to keep us safe and sound from the hazards of the jungle. We would pray for nothing to kill us, not the ferocious river, not the venomous snakes dangling from barks, or writhing on the ground. This jungle was infested with snakes, tarantulas, and many heinous creatures that were always on prey. As we prayed with each beat of our hearts, we remained safe.

There were young adults traveling with us as well, who were robust. They portrayed a force that depicted survival, but they happened to be the first ones to give in. In spite of them having the built requisite for survival, they fell weak. To witness all of this showed that true strength comes from prayers. When you pray, you know there is God. When you pray, you know God and His angels will protect you from all harm. Your mind hangs on to this thread of faith, and it is enough to keep you secure. Our prayers and faith have been one of the pillars of our survival.

My family and I had faith that we would reach Honduras. We already had endured the worst of it. We tethered through the raging oceans and escaped the clutches of lecherous men. If we had managed to come out alive and stronger from all those situations, then this jungle was nothing that would break our will to reach my brother. We knew we would see him and my step-father. We would all then set foot on a new journey to the U.S.

My mother was the greatest inspiration through this ordeal. She had this reassuring vision that we would make it alive. She believed that we would make it to the other side of the world. Her perseverance became our safety net, making me believe that we would climb out of this well of suffering and that we were only stranded for now, not forever. She is someone I am truly proud of. She has been the epitome of wonder, strength, fortitude, resilience, dominance, kindness, and life.

Cutting through that jungle was not limited to just these sights. There was more that I experienced, more things that left me perplexed and stunned. Remember my time from the old man's salon-shop house that was cockroach-infested? Well, compared to the cockroaches I saw in the jungle, the ones that were terrorizing me at night seemed like an infant to an adult. The cockroaches inhabiting the jungle were humongous. They were the size of my palms. Each time I saw one, I would feel my soul escaping my body.

The mountain that required two whole days to be conquered was where we lost one of the Indians. We had no means to trace his footsteps. He seemed to have disappeared completely. The other Indian did something equally deranged. He picked one of the tarantulas, a snake, and one of the ginormous ants and placed them on our fingers. Instead of fighting him back, we wondered why he was doing this. There was underlying comfort, knowing he must have a reason for doing this.

We were right. The Indian did what he did as a backup measure. He believed by allowing the poison to penetrate our skins; if either of us were to be attacked by these creatures during our journey, we would not be affected by the poison. It would fail to plunge us to our death as our immune system would have already accepted the venom. The entire process then turned out to be intriguing. The Indian had us lined up, and I was impatient to experience it.

Once the Indian made sure we were all vaccinated by the venom, he broke another news of dread to us. We were to vanquish yet another mountain. As he announced this news, we started to wonder how long would it take for us to reach our destinations. This was the point where things changed. This was the point where the Indian started to grow discerned and started to blabber in a different dialect. Observing the shift in his demeanor, daunted havoc upon us as well. He was a native Kuna Indian. Mustering the courage, the Indian finally acknowledged that we were lost.

Initially, no one reacted. No one dared to bulge a muscle in fear of losing the moment. Each pair of eyes was trained on the Indian. Each one of us waited patiently for him to tell us that he was only playing a trick. But as seconds turned into minutes, we realized the gravity of the situation. We were lost in the heart of a jungle that was menacing. My mother went berserk, and so did the other people. I recall the frail voices that were crying hysterically, but no one was there to hear us. We were stranded.

My mother fired questions at the Indian, asking how it was possible that we were lost when we had been walking for two days straight. She told him how we were starving, but that was not enough to solve the problem. We were famished, and bile kept on churning in our mouths. All of us were deeply affected by hunger, and people were fainting; even I fainted at some point. We had grown weak due to walking continuously for forty-eight (48) hours.

On the third day of this excursion, the Indian told us that he needed to climb to the top of the mountain again to see where we were. He also said he would hunt an animal so that we could all feast on it. My mother wondered what animal could he possibly hunt, but we were unable to question him due to our language barrier. The Indian did not speak the same variation of Spanish as we did. We were not familiar with his dialect, either. Nodding in agreement with him since arguing with him was not an option; we followed him up to another mountain where he hunted and slaughtered a large animal that resembled a cow. The animal had horns and was called Jabali in Spanish. Once the animal's blood ran dry, the Indian did not waste much time cooking it. Once cooked, we all devoured the meat. We were starving and chose to ignore the fact that the meat was a little raw. To have our first meal after days felt like pure bliss. The pleas of our stomach were finally heard and answered.

Once all of us had our energies restored, we continued trekking after the Indian to the top of the mountain. That was where he told us that we had walked in the opposite direction of our destination. Adding to our dilemma, what was meant to be a two-day trip ended up being a five-day trip. Five days of walking endlessly, five days of losing people with whom we had begun this journey, five days of walking around the river Pisa, treading its temper. Its rage took the lives of most, leaving behind only eight to ten of us.

The memoir of the jungle is forever scribed in my mind. In spite of the loss we suffered, in spite of the fatigue and sickness, in spite of having seen people drift away with the changing tide, I inherited the essence of life. I learned what survival means, to endure whatever is discarded your way, and to make the most of the cards you deal with. From our adults letting us children sit on their shoulders to them holding each other's hand and forming a human chain, we learned, to combat nature was not one man's task. But coming together, being united, we were able to withstand all odds.

The jungle taught me of togetherness, of fighting, and of losing it all at the end of the day. But with the morning comes a new opportunity that we have to claim. Else we would be stagnant. We have to keep moving forward in life. We have to accept everything and walk forward. If we refuse and sit in one place, we will perish. With perseverance, we managed to walk for five days straight until the trees started to clear away. No longer were the barks densely packed.

A pathway appeared before us, a reward for having suffered the monstrosity of the jungle. After crossing the mountains, we reached Nasser Red, a modest settlement of the Kuna Indians. The first thing I saw left me embarrassed and blushing red. The women were exposed. Their chest was bare, their breast hanging low. Men and women had their bottoms covered with an article of brown clothing that was minimal. That was all the clothing they had. Once I managed to overcome my initial unease, I took notice of how both the men and women had adorned their ears and noses with big gold rings. Another adornment of an oddity in common was how they had used dirt as make-up. Streaks of soil were lined across their cheeks and on their bodies.

For moments, I was lost, unable to contemplate the situation. These people were a part of civilization, yet they were roaming around just like that. Bare. Only their private areas covered. The Indian, who was with us, assisted us by translating everything and overcome the language barrier. My stomach was roaring again, and we had no food. In the hopes of curbing my hunger, I sat down on the ground and began clipping my nails with the nail-clipper I had carried all the way from home. There were these children running around me. Once their eyes settled on the nail-clipper, they turned erratic. It seemed they wanted the clipper. The air around me felt eerie out of the blues, and I had little choice but to surrender the nail-clipper to these children. It was the last time I saw my nail-clipper, my last memory of my home in Peru.

Feeling disheartened with hunger, I was about to pick up the dirt to eat when the same bunch of children returned. This time they returned with an offering. Their hands were filled with bread, water, lemon, and cocoa. This was not all that they had to offer. They extended an invitation our way. We were invited to their homes. To have the possibility of seeking shelter in someone's house for a while, we jumped at the opportunity and went over to their house. At first, I felt alienated since the children were continuously glaring at my nails, trying to wonder why I would clip them. Slowly, however, we both came to a mutual understanding that we were different.

These people turned out to be very hospitable. They brought forth food, and we spoke with one another in our own languages. It seemed we understood each other even when our words made little sense. One unusual thing I came to realize back then was their trade system. These people were not accustomed to using money to purchase something. They were only aware of bartering. Hence, when the children had taken my nail-clipper, they gave us food and their generosity in return.

We stayed at their accommodation for a little longer as sickness had started to nestle within our bodies. Their houses were no common establishment. Four trees were erected together, supporting a second story like a platform. They had carved holes within the bark of the trees to be used as ladders. Their reason for having erected their house high was the rain. They were aware that each time it would rain, their house would be flooded; hence, this was a preventive measure.

Having suffered several hardships in those five days, the effects started to show. From eating the bug-infested meat of the animal to having strained our muscles, we were sick and no longer able to continue our voyage immediately. It was a tree-house experience where I witnessed the blessing of rain without it weighing me down. The breeze was infinite, and the house was chilly due to the lack of insulation. Our stay was better than any five-star hotel experience, as it was what we needed the most back then. It was a blessing to be able to find accommodation in the midst of the wilderness.

This was not all about the kindness of those Indians. When we woke up on the morning of the day we were to leave, they had prepared for our journey. They were aware that we still had a long way to go and would be in dire need of food. Our eyes welled up, seeing the immense love and kindness they showered us with. This was only the first town of Panama that we landed on. The memory of that land is forever engraved in my mind.

The remembrance of those five days is still evident in my body. The scars on my body are the verification of what I had undergone. Even today, there are three holes in my body. However, instead of being saddened by them, I look back at them as my trophies. Those Indians showed me what it means to be human. Even when you have little, you share whatever you have with another soul in need because you do not want for another person to go through the pain of not having the basic necessities.

The memories of those five days are spiritual to me. I left the land of those generous Indians with a promise that one day I would return to meet them. Though I am yet to fulfill that promise, I do hope that one day I will get back to them and thank them for blessing me with acceptance and sheer kindness.

Chapter 7
More Traveling

From one country to another, we knew we had to push ourselves further. We were unfazed by boundaries or borders. The only thing that kept us moving was my brother and Richard, too, for my mother.

Our final destination was the U.S., but before we could have gone there, we had to make a stopover at Honduras. That stopover came with endless life lessons that shaped me to be the person I am today. We were all set to leave after recovering for a short getaway, which in today's time could be considered an exotic vacation for someone with influence and wealth, but for us, it was a means of recovery. Seeking shelter in the little town of Panama, my mother had managed to console herself. The requisite break allowed her to catch a breath and try to contact Richard.

The call to Richard was meant to inspire my mother to fight better, stand taller, and face all odds. The call was supposed to leave her feeling lighter. It was supposed to let her know that her son and lover were waiting for her. It was supposed to leave her knowing that all the decisions she took thus far were worth it all. Instead, the call left her rejected. A brutal rejection came when she only felt persuaded to go to Honduras. This was the point where my mother learned of my brother, Hozier. He was abandoned by Richard. Richard seemed to have allowed his doubts to prevail that we might never reach Honduras. He did not want to bear the liability of my brother. Thus, prioritizing his interest as he did not want to risk losing all of his money, he abandoned Hozier. My mother finally came face to face with Richard's true color. Hozier was placed in the custody of an adoption center, while Richard was en route to the U.S. by himself.

The news sufficed to pull the ground from beneath her feet. Not only my mother but my siblings and I also felt that we were falling off the mountain we had climbed just to get here. By now, I was aware of the living standards of an adoption center. Children were treated as if they were a disease. Our eyes glossed once more, and our hearts tossed and turned. Pain coursed through our veins blithesomely. The news was of absolute devastation. We wanted to reach Honduras at the earliest. Alas, there came another obstacle. We had no money. All that we had was spent to commute this far. Even the money Mr. Escobar's people had given us was spent. We had to use that money to give it to the Indian who helped us cut a path through the jungle. We were beyond devastated. The empire of our peace was in ruins, and we had to walk on the debris of our hope. Nonetheless, having seen how my mother was irrepressible, I knew she would contrive whatever voyage or barter to get us through this difficulty and retrieve Hozier as she did for us.

After spending the days in the little town, the time arrived for us to accept the change of events and find our way back to Hozier. But it seemed the Indians were not quite done surprising us. Their last gesture had left us astounded. They showed what it meant to be humane. They showed that often those who have little of their own are the ones to understand the despair of another better.

The Indians were aware that we did not have any money, and we were desperately in need of a convoy to get us through. They ushered us to a nearby river that was supposed to sail us through with minimum disruption. Through the humility of a canoe to the nobility of a bigger boat, we were crisscrossed from the river of Colombia to Panama with the Indian's assistance. Our journey was defined by the ongoing hostile situation of Colombia since it was the early 80s, a time doused in the influence of Pablo Escobar's doings. The killing was widespread, and if you were to get caught in the middle of an ongoing butchery, you would be among the corpses too. The Indians warned us to be meticulous with our actions. Security was heightened, and the borders were thoroughly monitored as the patrol officers would be combing for Escobar's people everywhere.

From our walk to our talk, everything had to be faked so as not to come off as suspicious, or else we would be pushed back a thousand steps we took to reach this far. The Indians instructed us critically on what we had to do to avoid getting caught. Because if we were to get caught, then, if not Columbia, it would surely have been the grounds of Peru we would be touching.

During the 80s, everyone was traveling from Colombia to Panama, some for the sole purpose of running away from Pablo Escobar. It was a breath of relief for us that our mother became acquainted with Mr. Escobar and his people were aware that we were only trying to get away from Colombia for a better life. Had things not been this way, had the people of Mr. Escobar not given us money, we would never have afforded the expenses to cross the virgin jungle. When we had set foot on the buoyant yet turbulent boat, we were told that the journey we were setting foot on was far unpredictable than what we had covered until now. As much as we were scared by the piece of information shared, I realized my family had been taking risks up till now, so why be petrified by the water? We had no other choice. This was the only way to reach Honduras.

We bid our goodbyes and climbed into a little wooden canoe that was occupied by other voyagers as well. As if we had not been through enough, we were handed another challenge to tackle. There was a significant hole in the boat. A hole! And what was resting next to it? A bucket. The entire situation was insane.

We were burdening this wooden canoe with our weights as it had to get the river across, embrace the ferocious tides of the ocean, and stream a ghastly river before we could reach another town. So, while the captain of the boat was navigating his vessel, we were all equipped with buckets instead of a paddle and clearing the water out continuously instead of waddling our way through the rough waters. If we were to stop, then our doom was imminent.

The entire sail was swaying up and down heavily. Each slump was momentous. The waves would lift the boat effortlessly and then thrust it back down without a care. All of this was happening within the blink of an eye. Even when all of the passengers were chattering with one another, it did little to diminish the fear gripping our hearts. It seemed each wave that was coming our way had one thing on its mind – to swallow us whole!

Finally, the time arrived when the river merged majestically with the ocean, and we abandoned the canoe to board a ship. Here a plan was made. We were reprimanded for lurking about this ship. Instead, we were to seek secrecy within the storage of the boat with other passengers. If the transition from the river to the ocean was insufficient for leaving me feeling sick, then this entire puzzlement of hiding not to have ourselves exposed surely did the deed. People around me and I were sick to our core. But I had to suppress my seasickness.

I did not have the luxury to reveal what I truly felt. Maybe I did not really understand the precise gravity of the situation. Time was ticking away like a bomb for us, and if the wrong wire was cut, everything was to explode and turn into ashes. It was a matter of night anyway, but the hours seemed to have stretched themselves into a lifetime. With the next sunrise, which was highly anticipated, we were to get back into a smaller boat and cover more waves. By midnight, we were to get back on a bigger boat until we would reach a town in Panama.

Even after reaching a Panamanian town, the situation was not as easy as it sounded. Although I kept mum, I fretted that my expressions would give it all away, and it would all be over for us. One particular thing we all had to be very careful about was our identity. If we were not to remain low-key, we would be sent back to our hometown. If we were not to tell anyone who we were or where we were from, then there was a chance for all of us to get paid by the government. I was unsure what the exact details were, but this was what we were told.

Seeing the crowd of people and all of them desperately trying to hide, my sisters Carolina, Judy, and I were unsure of how to cloak our presence entirely. My mother saw us fidgeting. We were nervous. She pulled us away from the other people. As we were pulling away from the sea of people, my mother bumped into this lady while her calm and composed demeanor was crumbling. My mother ended up confiding in the lady without hesitation. Her words stuttered, and her voice broke. My sisters and I were doing our best not to show a single hue of pain just not to end up going back to Peru.

My mother shared how we had to make it to other countries just to save my brother in Honduras. For the first time, she told another soul how the man she loved was the man to have left her son to fend for himself in the harsh conditions of the adoption center. Hysteric, I felt someone slicing my heart each time she sobbed. The remembrance of my brother was no less than salt being rubbed on our wound. This new stranger was listening calmly to my mother and crying along with us. From our jungle expedition to how my brother was suffering alone, the lady shared our pain with us. She saw how we were trying to make it one town at a time.

This lady could have turned us away, as we were just strangers to have met by chance. Only she did not. She welcomed us in her house as the Indians had done. She offered us help and became another angel we met on the way. The kindness she showered us with can never be repaid. We were to spend one day and night at hers and then find our way back to Honduras at dawn. But after dusk, she came with a jeep outside of her house. It was well after dark, and no one could see even a shadow. Bewildered by the grunts of the jeep, I recall huddling with my sisters, locking our arms with one another to form a barrier if harm was to befall us. The worried look of my mother still haunts me, as fear had us in its clutches. Had we been betrayed? Before we could have wondered enough or conceived a plan to sneak out of a back door into the wilderness of a new town, the lady barged in through her front door.

We were speechless. We were growing closer, but our body only returned to its normal state of perplex when she mirrored our pale faces. Sure enough, there was a jeep, but she was the one to have summoned it. Our minds were racing if we were to accuse her or beg her for mercy if she had reported us. Before any of such could have happened and the pounding of our hearts would have grown numb, she told us that the jeep was for us. It was a carriage she had paid for just to get us through with some other people to Panama City. We had blinked our eyes in the hopes of deciphering the situation. She was saving us.

The jeep was for us to cross the Panamanian border and enter Costa Rica. Once more, when our heart swelled with gratitude, we only had enough time to mutter a *thank you* and take our leave. We boarded this jeep with other passengers, our eyes all glossy with uncertainty. Our road trip from here only lasted for a day before the jeep came to a halt. We had little choice but to stop and walk all around the Sarita, which is a variation of a border patrol. Since we did not have verified papers to get us through the Sarita, the drivers told us we had to walk around it and avoid getting caught.

As if that was in our hands! But I could not scoff. Instead, I watched my mother nodding in affirmation. They told us how they would be waiting at the other side of the border for us and would not leave without us. This was our task; to reach the other end without revealing our identities. Being aware of our state, these people were better equipped with knowledge on how to make it through and shared their knowledge with us. Despite having been told on how to get through the Sarita, my family managed to get lost. Perhaps it was too much information, or we were nervous. Whatever it was, we were lost. Now we had to battle with the fear of losing our transportation as well as the fear of getting caught at any second. We were alone. The route we were to tread was worth five hours, but it took us twenty-four (24) hours. We knew something was awry. Having walked for so long under the sun without water and food, we started to lose our battle to fatigue. All I recall is being engulfed by the darkness, and seeing my mother collapsing to the ground before I did too.

The next morning as we stirred on the damp soil, a small silhouette started to appear before us. Slowly we blinked our eyes to take note of a little girl coming our way. Next to her was a horse. Baffled, we were only staring at her when she broke the silence in Spanish. She stated how "they" were looking for us. The thought of who was looking for us filled us with dread. What if the patrol officers were looking for us? We eagerly questioned the girl who was the '*they*' she was referring to.

Having walked on an empty stomach, we did not fathom for the jeep to be still waiting for us. Rather than answering us, the girl observed our confused expressions and went away to retrieve her parents. Thankfully, the couple was warm and sympathetic. They must have taken note of our disheveled state and came to our rescue. They took us to their home. There, we were treated with respect and compassion. The couple offered us a meal, and we gobbled it down greedily. Neither the taste nor the dish mattered at that moment. All that mattered was to hush the cries of our stomach.

The couple offered us a room to rest our heads, and we accepted it whole-heartedly. We knew we were in dire need of help. More than that, we were aware we still had a tedious journey before us. The couple proved to be what a savior is. They appeared out of thin air for us and helped us beyond measures, without ever questioning or judging us. After we rested, the couple placed my sisters, my mother, and me on the back of their horses and guided us to the right path where the biggest surprise awaited us.

The jeep was there. It had not left and was waiting for us. From the cheery 'you guys made it!' to the proclamation of how proud they were of us, I felt at ease. Irrespective of how these people were strangers, they treated us like family. The engine of the jeep roared once more, and we managed to cover the distance to Panama City. By now, we knew the journey ahead would be less hectic in terms of the landscape.

We would no longer be cutting through mafia-infested cities or unknown jungles. Our only troubles would be getting through authorities without a single cent in our pocket.

Once the sight of the buildings became clear in our vision, my mother went berserk once more. She was impatient to go and rescue Hozier. At the same time, she had to make sure my sisters and I were safe. Having come to Panama City previously, she had managed to make friends with some of the residents here. One of her friends kept us with her for a couple of hours, but the ticking of the clock was haunting my mother. She had to see Hozier. People say, 'don't let desperation maneuver you,' but the truth is we can never undermine the extent of another person's suffering.

Only a soul in anguish would know how excruciating the pain we went through was. My sisters and I were scampering on the streets, begging. Yes, we were begging for money. We had to take a bus to the border of Panama and Costa Rica to get to Hozier. For that, we needed money. Sadly, even as we cried and beseeched our woes, not one soul who was donned in clean clothes stopped to help us. My mother realized that the hearts of these people were of stone. They would not be bothered by our plight. Instead of wasting more time, she took us hurriedly toward the bus station. Naturally, my mother's friend and we had no money, yet my mother attempted to board the bus without a ticket. The bus conductor approached her, telling her how much she owed him. If it was someone else in her situation, they might have admitted defeat, but she only sought their assistance. She told them how she had no money on her, but there was a person waiting at the end of our route who would pay the cost of the tickets. We literally had no one anywhere waiting for us. She kept crying throughout the journey.

Her tears never ceased. Her thoughts threatened to suffocate her. Her mind was turning cynic. She was petrified for our safety and well-being. We had no money to afford water, let alone finding accommodation. Her hope was Richard, but he had betrayed her. If dealing with the betrayal was not hurting her enough, she had the remorse of jeopardizing her children's care. It seemed we were at a dead end.

Throughout this unintended chase that we were on, it seemed God wanted us to go through everything. Hence, each time we deemed for our situation to be ending, a path would open up as if a magical portal. Help would emerge out of thin air for us, and I could never understand the reason behind this. Each time we hit a dead end, another route would open up. Similarly, as we felt we would be thrown off the bus, a man was silently watching us and noticing my mother bawling her eyes out. She had repressed her tears from the back of her palm, shunning our tragedy from the rest of the passengers, yet this man had witnessed it all. Slowly, he approached her, startling us. She started to have a conversation with him, who decided to be our next rescuer. He offered to pay our tickets, and as she turned to thank him and ask for his name, he only shrugged the matter off. For the moment, we were at ease and accepted his kindness. Whatever worry was left, we deemed it fit to think of it once we would reach the borders.

Much to our surprise, as we were boarding the bus, the very same man came forth and approached us. The man really took us by surprise. He admitted how he was taking us with him to a hotel where he was staying, and there, a separate room was already booked for us. We were stunned. Words fell short to thank him, let alone acknowledge the entire situation. Not only this, before we could have bolted the hotel door behind us, the man graced us with another revelation. A jet would be awaiting us the next morning that would take us to Costa Rica. As promised, we woke up the next morning to make our way to the private jet without ever finding out who the man was who helped us immensely. Not only did he assist us to travel in secrecy, as we could not have used our passports anywhere (if we were to declare our identity at any port, the authorities would have reported my father back in Peru immediately, and my mother did not want him to be notified), but he also gifted us with enough money for a stay in a hotel.

This time around, however, my mother headed straight for a local Catholic Church. We were new, and she was inching closer to falling apart. Each day she would wake up with fear for Hozier. We were clueless if he was fine. She made her way to a local church, asking for help. Unlike the one we had previously visited, here we were accepted by one of the older women working in the church. The older lady was living with her daughter and children. Having narrated our unusual journey to her, she elongated our stay at her house from a few days to nearly a month. It seemed that even though we were strangers, we were bonded by humanity.

Our stay at the old lady's residence is unforgettable. After hearing all that we went through, I remember her antics to cheer us up. She used to sing lullabies and poems to us, about spiders and whatnot, trying to elevate our mood, boost our morale, and assure us that everything would be alright. She gave us new-found hope when we were feeling low. We spent a month at her, never once feeling we were guests. She made us feel at home while another one of the church members was tending to our documentation. Apart from being a leader at the church, the man worked for immigration as well. With his assistance, our documents were perfected to help us travel safely.

The one month we spent with the lady was enough for us to overcome the hardships we had endured so far. These people offered us food, shelter, clothing, trips around the neighboring cities, and love. It was their love that painted our horizon blue all over again before we were able to take a flight through it to Honduras.

The time finally arrived when we were in Honduras. With our palms sweaty and souls shuddering, we were ecstatic that we finally covered a distance that was our nightmare. We had overcome our fears. Now we had to find Hozier and find a way to get him out of the adoption center. The adoption center was the worst in all of Latin America. Children succumbed to their deaths due to food scarcity and consuming the polluted water there.

To add to our worries, my brother was unable to talk anymore despite him being four years older than me. He used to speak when we were with him, and our situation was normal. Having undergone the calamity of losing his way with us, he was scared due to which he was unable to communicate with anybody. What else to expect out of such a situation? Such a life is the damnation of any person, and he was just a child. His surroundings changed, he knew no one, he had no money, his atmosphere was eerie and cruel, and the only person he knew, Richard, had left him to fend for himself.

My mother was unsure how to get him out of the system. Another legal battle awaited her, and the mere thought of it was frustrating for her. Given our journey, it took us far too long. My brother was placed for adoption by foster care. Unaware of how she was fighting against all the odds just to reach Honduras, the system had assumed she was never coming back for him. She had to resort to fighting in the court, pleading her innocence by recalling her nightmares all over again. It was not easy to relive the horrific moments over and over, but she had to do it.

Meanwhile, I decided to stay back with my brother in the adoption center and help him with the food. It provided him with a little bit of comfort that he was no longer alone. Also, I was able to boil water for him. This was not the end of our new challenge. As my mother was battling with the court to regain custody of her son, I had to tend to both my brothers. I had to boil water for them and change the diaper of my youngest brother while watching the abhorring reality of other babies dying there. No one was aware of the truth of the adoption center.

The food and dirty water were causing diarrhea. So, I helped the assistants there boil water and change diapers. Despite being a child myself, I was tending to all these dying children. Even I fell sick there. My time at the adoption center made me thank God for everything that I had. Even though we were on the run and had no money, I was thankful to still have a family that cared for me. My mother finally managed to win the battle. No matter how much I thank God, it would never be enough. We were all united once more and left. Although we still had no money, we felt lucky to have left the adoption center. Unable to think of a solution soon, we paid heed to Mr. Escobar's suggestion that he gave us when we were at his residence. He had told us to ask for the Matta's family upon reaching Honduras and look for Claudia Matta.

Claudia Matta was the daughter of the infamous Juan Matta, the head of the mafia family of Honduras. In his country, however, he was a Robin-Hood like a figure. As much as he was involved in illegal activities and was a criminal, he was also the man behind the infrastructure of many schools and parks in Honduras. Nevertheless, we had to begin our search to reach Claudia Matta since Juan was serving time in prison.

Her house, as we found it, was more of a giant mansion. It was situated blocks and blocks away from the entrance. Everything was concreted, draped with cement. As we were entering her estate, we saw a limousine entering the gates and bodyguards flocking all around it. I remember being transfixed in my shoes. We were staring at her, as she was staring at us. We were quite unlike the other Latin Americans. We had blonde hair, fair skin, and blue eyes –

our mother's heritage, which gained us Claudia's attention. After moments had passed, she rolled her window down to question our visit. This was our cue. We told her that her address was shared with us by Mr. Escobar. He was the one who had told us to pay her a visit after reaching Honduras.

The mere confession was our ticket to enter the Matta estate. The more we chatted with Claudia, the more I discovered how humble she was. We exchanged our pleas and our struggle to escape to the U.S., and she shared the story of her father being sentenced to a lifetime in America. Regardless of his conviction, he had left behind a never-ending fortune to his daughter, out of which she shared a couple of thousand dollars with us. In turn, my mother only had to do one thing.

Claudia gave the money to my mother on one condition – a letter had to be delivered to her father at all costs in the U.S. The letter was sealed and safely tucked with other documents that I was garlanding around my neck in a little purse. We were clueless about what was scribed in the letter, but being its carriers rewarded us with a huge sum of money and diapers for my little brother. Unbeknown to what destiny had in mind for us, unaware of where we were to reside or work, we used the money in order to make our way to the border of Honduras and Guatemala. Things were strained, albeit less jarring for us. We were together and had enough money to afford our meals.

Before we could have crossed the border, we had to wait in an open area with my brother, who was wailing out loud. The area was open, but luckily it was past midnight. At one point, I was afraid we were going to get caught by the authorities, and then it would all be over for us. As much as I had missed my father, managing to come this far, I wanted to see my mother succeed and reach the U.S. We spent our time there praying. This time we had no shelter to hide in. All that filled my vision were large boulders, patches of grass, and skeletal palm trees.

My mind was constantly chanting, "Dear God, don't let them see us." The patrol officers were religiously making rounds around the border. We only had one last obstacle to cross, one last country before we would reach the U.S. I really did not want for all of this to be over for us. There came the point where we all had to bend down, as the guards were near with their flashlights flickering near us. Their eyes were trained in our direction, yet they seemed to have swept their gazes from above us. It was no less than a miracle. Thank God, my brother had stopped crying by then.

It seemed God's angel had sprawled a comforter of invisibility over us, as the guards walked right past us. We had enough time now to cross the border without being spotted. As we crawled our way across silently, my heart and soul were eternally in debt to God and all the people we encountered on our way this far.

Chapter 8
Mexico

"When you reach the end of your rope, tie a knot, and hang on."

–Franklin D. Roosevelt

Moving from one obstacle to another, we were drained yet blissful. Our energy was completely depleted. The only thing keeping us intact was this flickering hope. Whenever I look back at the journey my family and I commenced, I am astounded as to how strong a human being is. If someone asks me now to consider embarking on such an adventurous journey, perhaps I hesitate. But at that time, when life shoved me in that situation, I seemed to overcome every hindrance.

Every trial, every challenge, I faced headstrong with my family. Moving across from Peru to Honduras, Panama, San Jose, and all the many towns and cities between them, our bodies surely took the toll because of bugs in our system due to eating dirt, raw meat, and whatnot. I became well-versed with fatigue than knowing what it meant to be healthy. After nights and days of sleeping on concrete and soil, we finally crawled through the barbed wire borders before setting foot on the grounds of Mexico.

Had we not been through trials endlessly, we may foolishly have accepted victory here. We could have rejoiced, saying, *'Hey, one more country before we reach our destination!'* But by then, life had matured my siblings and me. We were numb. We were elevated too, but part of us was silently waiting for uncertainty to creep in. So, we looked across the barren land, before rejoining the families who volunteered to offer us shelter, food, and clothes.

I cannot emphasize enough that throughout our journey, we met people with opposing natures. Some disregarded our shadows. Others treated us just the same as their family. We were bonded by kindness and humanity. That whole emotion of chaste kindness was so pure that it could never be penned down enough.

Back in San Jose, a city that I will forever remember for its uncompromised hospitality and infinite generosity, as promised by the priest there, all our needs were catered. With the assistance of the church people, the old lady who would forever be our angel, and many others, I felt as if the journey in the middle had never happened. Only its remains are present in my memories to date. Crossing the scorching hot sand dusting the border of Guatemala and Mexico, we felt triumphant. Our journey was an obstacle by now. Every time we crossed one path, our hearts soared with courage.

Driven by the new-found adrenaline rush, we realized how close we were to our destination. Even the betrayal we incurred from Richard became less significant. Most of the time, after crawling through the border, my siblings and I continued our march next to our mother. Her shadow was enough to provide us with wafting comfort. Knowing that we were all finally together, I knew that whatever was to come our way next, we could surely tackle it. If we were to look at our situation through an overview, it was only one more destination that we needed to tread before we would make it to the U.S. Just one more country!

We were beyond ecstatic. I remember my mother yelping in joy at how we made it to Mexico as well. The heat of this new land was disregarded. Our achievement eradicated all emotions of defeat. It was because of our excruciating walk on barren grounds that we stumbled on kinder souls. These people were just swift to befriend my mother after hearing the incredible journey we experienced first-hand. They were amazed to see the survivors standing before them and showered us with sustenance. From shelter to food, the next few weeks after arriving in Mexico were made easy for us.

I had heard how those who lack luxury in their life know the worth of sharing. They know what it means to have little, and so they share their roof with the homeless. This I can vouch for. My family and I were homeless. We had run out of the money that was given to us. Our pockets were dusty, our throats parched, and our lips and feet cracked. I was so skinny that I could trace my bones beneath my skin. Surely, our stay for a couple of days in San Jose benefited us by stabilizing our immune system and extracting the bugs from our system. Nonetheless, we were still weak.

Here came the part where I witnessed how generosity was not divided by race, language, or religion. These people we collided with became our guiding light. They provided us with food, water, love, and shelter. They opened the doors to their houses and community for us, and soon we became part of another clan. They showed us what Mexican hospitality is by adding more chairs to their dining tables. They told us now that we were in Mexico, we would be eating a lot. And these words became their vow.

They were true to their words as I remember eating all around the clock. From rice to bean and leaves, I indulged in the wholesome, homey goodness of Mexican cuisine. All that I can share with you is that Mexican food is just as luscious and inviting as their hearts. Before my siblings and I knew it, we were gaining more than what we had lost.

Our hearts were brimming with joy. Well, let's just say we gained love in abundance. Apart from dining in constantly, I would go out in their compounds with my sibling and play with the local children there. One thought that surprises me is how language was never a barrier for us. Everyone seemed to know the language of love. We were able to communicate with the other in little of what we knew and vice versa. Thus, from gaining weight, the locals delighted us with another wonderment that aided us in moving forward.

I recall how the people were giddily listening to their national anthem thundering proudly through their TV screens and cascading through the open air. Goosebumps ran down my spine at the roaring pride. It was during this when one of the ladies turned to us and suggested how we should conceal our identity by acting like Mexicans. This would ridicule the option of being deported back to Peru when we would be crossing the Mexican borders. We were stunned at the suggestion. One of our worries was being deported back to Peru or any authority along the way, alerting our father, who was searching for us. I missed him; I missed my Dad and my home. I yearned to go back to him, albeit not alone. I wanted to go back with my entire family. On the contrary, having witnessed this excruciating passage of ours, part of me wanted to witness my mother win. Throughout the ordeal, there were times when she blamed herself for all that we went through. To ease this woe of hers, I wanted nothing more than to make it to the U.S. now.

To alleviate my mother from this emotional burden, we initiated a new phase in our lives – one that was enthralling and simply fun. To me, this seemed like a rainbow after being drenched in tormenting rain for so long. Soon our training began. We were being schooled to merge ourselves into Mexican culture, and I loved every single second of it. From inheriting a vast vocabulary that included words of good and bad nature to mastering the route to our local address and remembering the names of a school we never went to, along with the teachers who fictitiously taught us varying subjects in the local Mexican school. Now, whenever the national anthem would play, I would not only sing along with it, but I also knew the meaning of each stanza. From the different presidents that came into position to the local crops grown in Mexico and its turbulent political and economic conditions, every piece of information was now at my disposal. There came the point where no one could distinguish us to be non-natives. For weeks on end, we rehearsed our new identity only to avoid being deported to Peru. Once our new family deemed it safe for us to travel further, we set foot into another town, and then another, and another until we came to a temporary stop in Mazatlán, Sinaloa.

I can recall the scenic beauty of its alluring beaches. Men were jumping from the top of a rock into the crystal waters. Its coolness was radiating amidst the humidity. Our time there was short-lived, but it was an escapade for us. Our time there was nothing short of an exotic vacation before we moved forward to D.F, also known as Distrito Federal. The D.F was the capital of Mexico, now known as Mexico City. You see, while the rest of the world calls the capital of Mexico as Mexico City, the locals call it D.F.

In Mexico, we came across countless people who were just as amiable. We went from one church to another, even militant churches, but not one person shunned the doors of mercy on us. From food to clean clothing and shelter, we were offered the riches of a soul. The more people we came across, the more they showed how we were not a bunch of misfits. These people made our journey easier. All we had to do was ask, and this would be our only step to access humanity. From the local Fathers at the churches to others, they would patiently provide our mother with a listening ear. As she would narrate our passage, they would be left stunned, and we would look back in amazement ourselves.

How did we survive all of that? The harsh jungle, the inadequate adoption centers, and the legal system that was unjust. From our closest ones betraying us to letting go of our home in Peru and finding newer relations along the way, my heart would swell in pride, knowing my family and I had surpassed all odds. My stay in Mexico is still alive in my mind. Each place I visited left its impression on my mind. It is not easy to surrender such beautiful and picturesque memories. I only want to hold on to these memories with all my heart and soul.

One such town I was in was Guadalajara. The patrons of the local church there extended their courtesy by taking us even to shopping. The mall they took us to was amazing. It left me baffled. These people selflessly presented us with lavish clothing and treated us to a dining experience that showed us that we deserved happiness too. As much as my mother wanted to deny it, along the lines of this journey, she may have deemed herself a culprit for our *exile*. She blamed herself internally for all the hardships we had to face, even when I was glad that I was with her and my siblings. And that's why being treated kindly by these people placed ease on her heart. I knew she was untroubled to see my siblings and me living happily.

These people were from the same Church we grew up in, which was Neo-Catholic Cathedral. The time came when we had to bid our farewells and make our way to our next destination that was Hermosillo. Every time we had to part ways with people who treated us like family, the moment was bitter. The only sweetness that I could extract from it was the chance to have known a pure soul. All of these people impacted my life greatly and taught me the art of selflessness.

As we moved to Hermosillo, which is rather close to the border, we had a one night stay at one of the motels there. This was all that we could afford. Our survival until now was heavily reliant on philanthropy. Hence, we were unable to afford another night at the motel and left the safety of the room the very next day. By the time we left the motel to visit the nearest church, it was high-noon. We were making our way to the church to scour some aid, contently knowing our nightmares were in the past now. I assume we had birthed our wishful thinking a little too early because as soon as we arrived at the local church, our worst nightmare was already present there.

You see, life has this tendency to make us face a challenge when we least expect it. It is a test for us to see if we repeat our mistakes, or if we have the heart to forgive another soul that once hurt us beyond measures. God tests us to see whether or not we have learned our lessons from the trials he put us through. These tests are dependent on the choices we make to help us see where we stand in life and move on. This test of ours came in the shape of Richard, whom I disliked with every fiber in my body. What was he doing here? Had he not made it to the U.S.? Was he aware we would be coming here? My mind was bustling with questions, and only one was answered. My mother seemed to be in a trance as Richard walked our way. This was all it took. This was all he needed before he managed to obtain forgiveness from my mother. Of course, he apologized after coaxing her for hours. It was beyond my understanding of how she forgot each and every one of his antics. To forgive someone is one thing, but to accept them back after they stab you in the back is another. There were too many mistakes of his to deem him the culprit. If none of them was enough, then was he abandoning her son alone not enough to allow him back in our lives?

All that Richard repeated was him being sorry and doubting my mother's ability to survive. He cried to her how he was wrong for not being hopeful that she would make it back eventually. She was hurt, and tears were profusely rolling down her cheeks. She had asked him his reasons for abandoning Jose in the adoption center, a question that should have reminded her not to accept Richard back. But he only used it to his advantage. He said he thought Jose was better off in the adoption center since he was unable to afford their expenses.

Richard masked his wrongdoings to be a sacrifice, making him able to woo my mother once more. Each of his mistakes was forgiven and forgotten. It was given for my mother to act in such a manner since she was in love. This statement sounds rather harsh, but this is the truth. You see, when we love someone, this sentiment within us conceals all the flaws of the other person. And it should be this way because we all have our flaws as well that we want hidden. But this love of ours should only help us accept the flaws of one another, not their selfish nature.

Richard had proven time and time again that he was unreliable. But my mother's feelings for him seized her ability to see his true colors. As she accepted him back, all I could think of was that he was untrustworthy. This strength of mine, to be able to see the true colors of a person, has helped me make endless critical decisions later on in my life. I am thankful to him for this, for teaching me how to see beneath the mask each one of us wears. After all, the true intentions of a person lay hidden behind their charades.

I am not criticizing the act of forgiveness. Oh no. It is important for us in order to heal whatever tragic wound our souls bear. Once we do it, only then can we accept our lives as they are. And that is what brings about peace. But to forgive someone does not mean you give them another chance to hurt you. Hence, when my mother accepted Richard back, I resented her decision. I ended up being one of those children who are always frowning, and I had all the reasons to do so.

I had to pretend to accept this person I hated. Alas, I had little choice than to be obliged to all the decisions my mother was making. I quietly bowed down to the decisions she made, even if they made me unhappy. Once she accepted Richard, she was happy, and I could see this glistening of relief in her eyes. With him now, we made our way back to the motel and his room. We were left to occupy ourselves with the cereal there was in his room while being envious of the company he was receiving of my mother. We also wanted her attention. She was our Mom.

As much as I wanted my mother to myself, I slowly discovered to be accepting of the entire situation. She was happy, and I wanted nothing more than that for her. She had endured a lot with my father, and if Richard made her happy even for the moment, then I wanted this happiness for her. Come to think of it; it is better to have the company of a man.

No matter how much we deny it, there are times and situations when the company of a man can do you good. Even in my own world as a child where I was fighting all monsters alone, I knew Richard's company would do us good if we were ever barricaded by robust men.

After having settled down in the motel room with Richard, we went to visit one of the patrons that my mother had befriended from church. They had graciously shared their address with us. When we reached the given address, I saw a house that I can never forget. As I was walking in the house with my family, I recall seeing a black dot flying right past me. The more I stared, the bigger the dot grew until I understood it was a roach who was flying like an airplane before me. Just like an airplane, it came to land in the middle of my forehead, assuming for my skin to be its runway.

I was yelling uncontrollably and running around, flailing my arms. Then the horror began. The cockroach went under my shirt. That was when my cries grew frantic. I was screaming on top of my lungs for help. My little sister was quick to come to my rescue and started hitting me with her doll that was made out of fabric. She was hoping to put the cockroach out from my body, but the more it wriggled, the more berserk I grew. Finally, the cockroach decided to slip from under my shirt and crawled away as if nothing had happened. I breathed an air of relief, but my heart drummed wildly. It was puzzling how I was not afraid of the cockroaches in the jungle, and yet this one terrified me. This marked the end of entertainment for everyone, and once my mother had met the person we came to meet, we made our way back to the motel to take some rest. The next morning, Richard and my mother decided to leave, leaving us to consume the cereal we were eating on a daily basis with milk. Despite having to eat cereal every day, we were thankful for the meal. It was better than sleeping on an empty stomach or eating infected meat.

Once we had eaten, we were quick to get dressed and leave. Our next destination was a church located near El Paso, the border of the U.S. and Mexico. This was the moment of truth for us, the 1st of September. All of our rehearsals of being Mexican were to be used there. The only obstruction now was *how*. How were we to cross the border? Our minds were constructing an obstacle course of the highs of a mountain and the lows of a fierce river. One wrong move, and we would be pulled into a deep mess.

Mustering our courage and realigning our wits, my mother decided to confide in the American priest, who was fluent in Spanish as well. She was maintaining her calm, but even then, the shiver was evident in her voice. I can never forget the day when she was absolutely vulnerable. It so happened to be my birthday as well. Yes, it was my birthday, but I doubted if anyone would remember, given our situation. She confessed to the priest how she wanted to cross the border but did not wish to risk our lives. She was not traveling alone; after all, she had us– her children.

I remember the gaze of the priest, how it was switching from my mother to our faces. He must have seen how helpless we were. All of our frowns were indented across our foreheads to shield our terror. He could have said no and left us completely hopeless, but God softened his heart.

"Don't worry…" He paused.

That one second the priest took, it felt as if we lived a lifetime in it. Finally, he affirmed his assistance. Only when he said he would offer us help, I felt my body gaining consciousness again. My mother was in tears, a smile playing on her lips before she turned to look my way with a huge smile on her face. She shared the news I thought no one remembered. She said it out loud that it was my birthday. Everyone else seemed to remember then. The priest, too, looked euphoric. He told us he had baked a cake that morning on a whim. With a grin on his face, he went to the kitchen and came back with a cake in his hand. Soon we all busted singing, 'Happy Birthday.' The entire atmosphere changed from thick tension that was suffocating us to this liberating air that gave us courage. That birthday was a gift from God for me. It was one of the best birthdays I have lived thus far, and why shouldn't it be? We rejoiced, celebrated, and devoured the scrumptious cake before the priest returned with a set of clean clothes for us to change. As he handed us the clothes, he swallowed a lump in his throat.

"You guys are white?" He questioned.

"Yes?" My mother answered reluctantly.

"Well, you don't look like Mexicans. You have fair skin, blonde hair, and blue eyes. This shouldn't be hard for you guys to cross the border. They will know you are not Mexicans. In fact, you look like Americans. This shouldn't be so hard."

The priest laughed and eased our tensed muscles. He went on to amaze us further. He concealed our appearance to be that of tourists. I kid you not when I say this: He dressed us up from big backpacks, tourist shirts, and hats. We were doused in an array of colors to give off the impression that we were only visiting. Our next set of instructions was concise yet unnerving. He told us to barge into the border as if we lived there. We should not be giving away our unease.

Of course, the news struck my mother with a revelation that made her feel queasy. It was the last border we had to cross and naturally the hardest. Her palms were sweaty as she exclaimed loudly how this was going to be worse than all that we had suffered to this point. Watching her overwhelmed, our minds were filled with fear too. We knew one slight mistake would take us back to where it all began. After all, it was the border of the United States that we were talking about. Our stakes were at an all-time high there.

Slowly, we started to snake our way to the border, which was a prolonged stretch of iron bars and grills. The entire momentum was comical, how people were standing at both sides of these gates, wanting to cross over. Just then as we were sweeping the entire area, we saw how a man was cloaking this hole he seemed to have cut through the gates and charging people money just so that they could crawl through it. Clearly, the man must have been making a lot of money since what he was doing was dangerous. Watching such a sight made me anxious. I could feel my body running cold and sweating.

My mum was astounded, wondering if that was the border, a doubt that I generously cleared for her. I shared with her how it was just one part of the border, and there must have been another gate for us to cross once we navigated through this. We were mumbling and questioning among ourselves, a sight that was hysterical for the priest. Settling ourselves with answers about the border, we finally approached the man behind the hole in the gate. That was when we were struck with another worry. How were we going to pay him thousands of dollars?

"Listen, you need to let these people go." The priest stepped in before us and took the man next to the hole by surprise. We were all amazed to see the priest interfering for our sake. "I know you're the one who carved this way out, but you have to do me this favor and let them go. Please, it's my request." The father patted his pocket before fishing out an object that resembled a watch and gave it to the man. "They are my people, I know them. You have to let them go and not charge them. Just them, please I request you."

The man instantly seemed to bow before the priest and agreed to each word he said. This is one thing about the Mexicans, in spite of their profession, they are very respectful toward a religious figure. With that, we entered the border with a breeze. No money was charged and no risk of getting caught either. The entire moment resembled a stroll in the park. Disbelief took us as we slowly turned to face what was the border of Mexico we had crossed. With the blink of an eye, we were standing on American soil.

We turned to face the priest with misty eyes, and our lips twitched in a smile. He seemed to be reciprocating our emotions as he gave us the directions to the nearest church. Slowly, the distance between him and us started to increase as we moved away from what was Mexico. As we started traveling on the American side of the border, our surroundings began to transform. Neat houses, aligned in a symmetrical line, started to fill our vision as we followed the directions given to us before entering the first church we came across.

Over there, my mother wasted no time and contacted her sister Alicia, her brother Tony, and her uncles. My mother was in tears as she called her family, and they assured her they would be coming to take us home soon. It seemed a huge burden was lifted off our shoulders. Our souls felt feather-like as we finally basked in the freedom. All day long, we waited in the church, crying and listening to the masses obediently. Time was not frozen, but it passed slowly. Each hour that passed, we counted every minute of it. Soon the time came for the church to close, but we knew we could not leave. My mother's family was coming to pick us up.

Once more, we were met with soft words as my mother shared with the clergy how her family was coming to pick us up. They offered her to make another call, on which she was told they would be arriving soon since they had left the very second after her first call. Our wait continued while seated in the church office. After several minutes of fidgeting, our attention was disrupted. As scurrying footsteps echoed down the hallway, she left her chair to run before a sob escaped from her. We knew they were there.

Unknown faces filled our vision. People who were our family finally met us. By exchanging hugs, I knew I was home. It was odd how I had never seen these people before. I had cousins, some who did not know Spanish, and some who could speak a little. I met my cousin Michelle who could only speak English. Seeing her, I wondered at that moment if I would ever be able to learn this language. Then I met Chris, my other cousin, who had just finished learning Spanish. It felt simply good to be able to talk to someone who could understand us.

Finally, we were taken home. Not our own home but that of our aunt, yet that sentiment of being where we were was supposed to settle within us. Like a soft candle flame, we melted into acceptance, and this life we had been chasing. From the mountains that we had climbed to the oceans we had floated on, our feet finally accepted a solid ground. That was where our epic journey came to a stop.

I, however, knew that this was only the end of another chapter in the book of my life. If I were to flip a few pages, I would see myself riding my own bike to school from our house six months down the road. My family was given this beautiful canvas. I knew we would be painting it soon with our new beginnings.

HOW I WAS ABLE TO HEAL MY TRAUMAS

www.ingramcontent.com/pod-product-compliance
Lightning Source LLC
Chambersburg PA
CBHW021146090426
42740CB00008B/965